BURT FRANKLIN: BIBLIOGRAPHY & REFERENCE SERIES 497

AN INDEX & BIBLIOGRAPHY TO

Douglas C. McMurtrie's

A History of

PRINTING

IN THE

UNITED STATES

AN INDEX & BIBLIOGRAPHY TO

Douglas C. McMurtrie's

A History of

PRINTING

IN THE

UNITED STATES

With a Checklist of Bibles, Checklist
of Almanacs, and a Geographical Checklist of Serials

Prepared by
EMILIE QUAST

BURT FRANKLIN, *Publishers*
New York

Published by Burt Franklin, Publishers, 235 E. 44th St., N.Y. 10017
Copyright © 1974, Lenox Hill Publishing & Distributing Corporation.

Published by LENOX HILL Pub. & Dist. Co. (Burt Franklin)
235 East 44th St., New York, N.Y. 10017
Reprinted: 1974
Printed in the U.S.A.

Burt Franklin: Bibliography and Reference Series 497

Library of Congress Cataloging in Publication Data

Quast, Emilie.
    An index & bibliography to Douglas C. McMurtrie's A history of
printing in the United States.

    1. McMurtrie, Douglas Crawford, 1888-1944. The history of printing in the
United States—Indexes. I. McMurtrie, Douglas Crawford, 1888-1944. The history
of printing in the United States. II. Title.
Z208.M172   016.6862'0973   74-5200
ISBN 0-8337-5495-5

Contents

	PAGE
INDEX	7
BIBLIOGRAPHY	49
CHRONOLOGICAL CHECKLIST OF BIBLES	73
GEOGRAPHICAL CHECKLIST OF ALMANACS	77
GEOGRAPHICAL CHECKLIST OF SERIALS	81

INDEX

AN INDEX AND BIBLIOGRAPHY TO DOUGLAS C. McMURTRIE'S HISTORY OF PRINTING IN THE UNITED STATES

Abáellino, the Bravo of Venice, by Zschokke..................214
Abällino, der Grosse Bandit, by Zschokke.....................214
Abbey, Dorephus...................180
ABC with the Shorter Catechism, The.............................90
Account of the Conversion of the Reverend Mr. John Thayer, An.355
Account of the Pelew Islands, Situated in the Great South Sea, An.............................218
Account of the Siege of Savannah, by the French and Rebels, Commanded by Count D'Estaing and General Lincoln...............391
Act for Ascertaining the Rates of Foreign Coins in her Majesties Plantations in America, An....13
Act for Ascertaining the Rates of Money for Payment of Debts....13
Act for Granting to their Majesties the Rate of One Penny per Pound upon the Real and Personal Estates within / N.Y. /......130
Act for opening and extending the navigation of the Potomack River, An...................300
Act for opening and regulating the Superior Court in the Several Counties of / Georgia /......383
Act for the better Settling of Intestates Estates...........383
Act of 1791 (Libel, English).....149
Act to Incorporate the Society of the Lying-In Hospital of the City of New-York, An.........215
Adams & McDuffee.................190
Adams & Niles...............248, 250
Adams, Charles C. 189-90, 199
_____. & Co. 189-90
_____. (widow)..............190
Adams, James...126, 233, 236, 244-51
_____ and Sons (firm).......248
Adams, James Jr. 248, 250

Adams, John (president)......213, 264-65
Adams, John (printer)126, 248-50, 252-53
Adams, Samuel........126, 248-50, 252-53
Adamses & Smyth (firm)................250
Adancourt, Francis..............197, 211
Addington, Stephen....................215
Addison, Joseph......................374
Address of the Convention of the Representatives of the State of New-York to their Constituents, An...181
_____ (Dutch edition)..............181
Address of the Representatives of their Majestyes Protestant Subjects, in the Province of Mary Land Assembled 101
Address to the Citizens of Philadelphia, Respecting the Better Government of Youth, An, by Matthew Clarkson.........................95
Address to the Inhabitants of North Carolina . . , by Wallace Borden.338
Address to the People of the United States, by George Washington..252-53
Adolphus, Gustavus....................221
Adultress, The........................272
Advice of Evan Ellis, . . . The......246
Adviser Glen's Falls, N.Y...........220
Advocate of the People, Auburn, N.Y..176
Aesop's Fables........................374
Affecting History of the Captivity and Suffering of Mrs. Velnet.........202
Agricultural Museum, Georgetown, D.C.274
Aikman, Alexander...................328-29
Aikman, Alexander Jr..................329
Aikman & Douglass....................329
Aikman, William.......................329
Aitken, Robert........................67
Albany Argus, N.Y..179-80, 186, 198, 213
Albany Centinel, N.Y....178-79, 189, 211
Albany Chronicle: or, Journal of the Times,.N.Y..............177-78, 196
Albany Gazette, N.Y..............163, 172
Albany Gazette, N.Y. (2d).........174-77 179-80, 193
Albany Journal: or, The Montgomery,

Washington and Columbia Intel-
  ligencer, N.Y.................174-75
Albany Register,N.Y.176-77, 179-80, 187
Albrecht, Johann......................80
Alexander, Caleb. Young Ladies' and
  Gentlemen's Spelling Book........193
Alexander, James...........143, 145, 148
Alexandria Advertiser, Va.......268, 301
Alexandria Daily Gazette, Va.........301
Alexandria Expositor, Va......273, 301-2
  moved to D.C......................302
Alexandria Times, Va.................301
Alfonso, King of Castile, by Matthew
  G. Lewis..........................272
All the News for Two Coppers,
  Philadelphia, Pa...................62
Allen, James..........................97
Allen, Solomon, Jr...................176
Allen, William.......................33
Allied Mercury, Phila, Pa......... 86-87
Almanacs: see under specific name or
  see List of Almanacs by Location.
Amen, David..........................305
Amen, J. & D. (firm).................305
American, Indiana, Pa.................98
American, The, Fayetteville, N.C.....360
American Accomptant, The, by
  Chauncey Lee......................197
American & Daily Advertiser, Balt.Md.128
American Chronicle, NYC...............152
American Citizen, NYC................204
American Crisis, The, by Thomas
  Paine.............................181
American Daily Advertiser, Phila.59, 363
American Eagle, Sag Harbor, L.I......203
American Eagle, Catskill, N.Y.......,203
American Farmer, Poughkeepsie, N.Y.
                               189, 190
American Gazette, Norfolk, Va........294
American Geography, By Jedidiah Morse239
American Literary Advertiser, D.C....267
  Moved to Alexandria, Va..........267
American Magazine, Phila., Pa..16, 38-39
American Magazine, NYC...............162
American Magazine and Monthly
  Chronicle, Phila., Pa.............56
American Magazine, or General
  Repository, Phila., Pa............56

American Monitor, Plattsburg, N.Y.219
American Preceptor, by Caleb
  Bingham.........................212
American Primer, Improved ... .203
American Reader, by Herman Daggett187
American Reader, by John Hubbard..212
American Spelling Book, An, by
  Asa Rhoads.....................218
American Spelling Book, by Noah
  Webster........................212
American Spy, Lansingburgh, N.Y.
                 175, 196-97, 207
American Watchman, Wilmington, Del.
                                252
American Weekly Mercury, Phila., Pa.
  14-16, 20, 30, 37, 112, 279, 310
Americanische Staatsbothe, Der
  Lancaster, Pa...................80
Americanus, Sylvanus, pseud. see
  Samuel Nevill
Anderson, John....................152
André, John.......................181
Andrews & Brynberg................251
Andrews, Ebenezer T...............178
Andrews, Loring................178-79
_____. & Co...................178
Andrews, Samuel...................251
Andros, Sir Edmund (N.Y. Gov.)
                           134, 137
Angell, James...............124, 127
Animadversions on a Late Publica-
  tion, Entitled, the Duty and
  Obligation of Christians to
  Marry Only in the Lord, by
  Stephen West...................181
Animadverstions on James Holland's
  Strictures on General Dickson's
  Circular Letter of the First of
  May, 1800.................363, 365
Anno Sexto Annae Reginae An Act
  for Ascertaining the Rates of
  Foreign Coins in her Majesties
  Plantations in America.........13
Antigua Gazette, Antigua..........44
Apollo, D. C.....................270
Apollo; or, Chestertown Spy, Md...131
Apollo Press................270, 272
Appeal from the Twenty eight Judges,

to the Spirit of Truth and true
Judgment in all faithful Friends
called Quakers, that meet at
this Yearly Meeting at Burling-
ton, the 7 month, 1692, An, by
George Keith...................8, 136
Archibald, Robert...................361
Argus; and New Jersey Centinel,
    Bridgeton, N.J...................243
Armbrüster, Anton..........22, 33, 47-49
Armbrüster, Anthon..................119
Armbrüster, Gotthard.............47-48
Armstrong, Alexander................95
Arnett & Hodge.....................352
Arnett, Shelly..............237, 239-40
Arnett's New-Jersey Federalist, New
    Brunswick, N.J...................239
Arnold, Benedict..................66, 123
Associate Reformed Church............208
Atkins, Samuel, Kalendarium Pennsil-
    vaniense, or, America's Messenger..2
Atkinson, Thomas....................97
Atlantic World, D.C.................272
Augusta Chronicle and Gazette of the
    State, Ga........................394
Augusta Gazette, Ga................394
Augusta Herald, Ga.................398
Aurora, Phila., Pa.................269
Autobiography, by Benjamin Franklin
        20-21, 28, 32, 34, 39, 41-42

Babcock & Hickock.............194, 197
Babcock, John (Johannis).175-6, 194, 196
Bache, Benjamin Franklin.............53
Bache, Richard.....................122
Backus & Whiting...............179, 189
Backus, Eleazer F..................179
Bacon, Francis.....................374
Bacon, Thomas....................115-16
Bailey & Stewart....................79
Bailey, Francis..................79-80
Bailey, Jacob.......................80
Baillie, _____ 367
Baker, John........................98
Balance, Hudson, N.Y...........191, 203
Balance Advertiser, Hudson, N.Y...191-92

Balance and Columbia Repository,
    The, Hudson, N.Y.........191, 192
Balance, and New-York State Jour-
    nal, Albany, N.Y..............192
Balance Press, Hudson, N.Y........193
Balch, Rev. Stephen Bloomer.......258
_____ . A Series of Letters . . .
    to the Rev. Adam Freeman......271
_____ . Two Sermons, on the
    Certain and Final Persever-
    ance of the Saints............258
Balentine & Webster...............173
Balentine, Solomon.............173-74
Baltimore Daily Advertiser, Md....127
Baltimore Evening Post, Md........127
Baltimore Intelligencer, Md......128
Baltimore, Lord (1st)..........99-100
                    101, 103, 104
Baltimore, Lord (2d, Cecil Calvert)
                    99-100
Baltimore, Lord Charles...........112
Baltimore Telegraphe, Md.....128, 275
Baltimore Weekly Magazine, Md.....128
Barber & Schultz..................212
Barber & Southwick................176
Barber, John..................176, 253
Barber, Joseph W.............204, 212
Barber, Robert, & Co..............176
Barclay, Greek Grammar............374
Barnes, D.H., ed. Cicero's De
    Officiis......................187
Barnum & Jacacks..................190
Barnum & Nelson...................190
Barnum, Charles P.................190
Bartgis & Roberts..................86
Bartgis & Willcocks...........86, 303
Bartgis, Matthias.79-80, 86, 129, 303
Bartgis's Federal Gazette, Freder-
    icktown, Md...................129
Bartgis's Maryland Gazette, Freder-
    icktown, Md...................129
Bartgis's Republican Gazette, Fred-
    ericktown, Md............129, 305
Barton, Thomas.....................82
Bates, Isaac......................214
Bauman, Joseph.....................77
Bausman, Lottie. A Bibliography of
    Lancaster County..............78

Baxter & Wilson.....................294
Baxter, Daniel................260, 294
Baxter, Francis M...................335
Baxter, Richard. The Saints' Ever-
    lasting Rest...................217
Bayard, James A., Jr................274
Bayard, Nicholas....................135
Beach, Cyrus, & Co..................219
Beasley & Wills.....................361
Beasley, Joseph.....................361
Beaumont, William...................95
Bee, Hudson, N.Y...............192, 193
Bee, New London, Conn...............192
Bee, NYC............................192
Beecher, Lyman......................202
Beecher, Henry Ward.................202
Beissel, Conrad..........67, 70, 76-77
_____. Urständliche und Erfahrungs-
    volle Hohe Zeugnüsse............77
Beleurgey, Claudius.................335
Bell, Robert........................67
Bellew, John...................355, 356
Berkeley, Lord John.................221
Berkeley, Sir William (Va. Gov.)100, 276
Berry, John.......................97-98
Berwick, _____...................37
Bible: see List of Bibles by Date
Bill, James.........................203
Billings, Nathaniel.................210
Billmeyer & Leibert.................76
Billmeyer, Michael..................76
Bingham & Krider....................361
Bingham, Caleb. American Preceptor...212
_____. Columbian Orator..........212
Bingham, Lemuel.....................361
Black, _____.....................360
Black & North.......................243
Black, John. Examination of the Rev-
    erend John Anderson's Discourse
    on the Divine Ordinance of Sing-
    ing Psalms.......................86
Black, William............236, 252, 253
Bladen, William................105, 107
Blanchard, _____...........352, 359
Blauvelt, Abraham...............239-40
Blauvelt & Arnett...................239
Bliss, Luther,......................197
Bliss, Pellatiah....................211

Blodget, Samuel. Thoughts on the
    Increasing wealth and National
    Economy of the United States
    of America.....................271
Bloodless Revolution (Eng., 1688)
                           101, 134-35
Blutige Schau-Platz oder Märtyer-
    Spiegel, by Tieleman Jans Van
    Braght..........................77
Boden, Elizabeth....................333
Boden, Nicholas.....................326
Böhm, Johann...............33, 47, 48
Bolting Act of 1678.................134
Bomb Search'd And found stuff'd
    with False Ingredients, by
    Caleb Pusey.....................12
Bond, Thomas...................258, 300
Bonnetheau & Evans..................334
Bonnetheau, Gabriel M...............334
Bonsal & Niles......................251
Bonsal & Starr......................251
Bonsal, Vincent................128, 251
Book of Common Prayer...5-6, 138, 140
Book of Knowledge Treating of the
    Wisdom of the Ancients, by
    Erra Pater, W. Lilly, tr.......206
Bookbinding....................72, 114
Borden, Wallace. An Address to the
    Inhabitants of North Carolina.338
Bordley, Thomas.....................109
Bowell & Black......................360
Bowell, A. F........................360
Bowen, _____.....................218
Bowen, _____.....................355
Bowen & Howard......................355
Bowen, Richard................126, 303
Bowen, Thomas Bartholomew....333, 334
Bowman & Potter.....................187
Bowman, Godfrey.....................187
Bowman, Parsons & Potter............187
Boyd, Adam.................349-51, 355
Boyd, John..........................90
_____ widow......................90
Boylan, Abraham H...................363
Boylan, William....354, 358, 360, 363
Boylan's North Carolina Almanac...354
Bracken, Henry. The Gentlemen's
    Pocket Farrier..................95

Brackenridge, Hugh Henry....87-88, 90
                              91, 92
_____ . Gazette Publications...90
_____ . Modern Chivalry........91
Bradford & Burgess................272
Bradford & DeForest...............150
Bradford & Rittenhouse..............7
Bradford & Zenger.................142
Bradford, Andrew..13-20, 24-6, 28, 30
                  32, 37-9, 55, **108**-9
                  138, 140, 310
_____ . 1st wife.................55
Bradford, Cornelia Smith.......16, 55
Bradford, Elizabeth Sowle...........1
Bradford, Fielding..............90-91
Bradford, John.....................91
Bradford, Moses...................252
Bradford, Samuel Fisher........56-57
Bradford, Thomas............56-57, 60
Bradford, William.................272
Bradford, William....................1
Bradford, William I...1-9, 12, 14, 16
                  20, 24, 25, 28, 50, 55-6
                  103, 108, 124, 135-42,
                  149, 150, 172, 222--227
_____ . Proposals for the Print-
    ing of a Large Bible..........5-6
_____ . daughter................138
_____ . 1st wife................138
_____ . 2d wife...........138, 141
Bradford, William II.....55, 138, 141
Bradford, William III ("Colonel")
                  16, 55-56, 60-61, 66, 152
_____ . Wife, nee Budd..........56
Bradford, William IV...............56
Braght, Tieleman Jans van. Der
    Blutige Schau-Platz oder
    Märtyrer-Spiegel...............77
Brandmüller, Johann................82
Bransford, Robert Mosby...........304
Bray, Thomas. The Necessity of an
    Early Religion................107
Brendle, William...................97
Breyvogel, Jacob D.................83
Brief Narrative of the Case & Tryal
    of John Peter Zenger, Printer
    of the New York Weekly Journal,
    A..............................148
Briggs, _____ 258

Brigham, Clarence S. Bibliography
    of American Newspapers........48
                  97-98, 246, 253, 305-6
Brokaw, Abraham...................208
Brooklyn Minerva & Long Island
    Advertiser, L.I..............217
Brown & Gilmore...................64
Brown & Sample...................97
Brown & Snowden............268, 301
Brown, Andrew.....................162
Brown, Benjamin...............94, 97
Brown, John. Dictionary of the
    Holy Bible..................92-93
Brown, Matthew......126-27, 268, 301
Brown, Samuel.....................152
Brown, Samuel R...............213-14
Brown, William................64, 66
Browne, John...................135-36
Brownejohn, Thomas...............190
Brownsville Gazette, Brownsville,
    Pa............................98
Bruce, David.....................327
Bruce, George....................327
Bruce, Robert....................333
Bruederschaft (imprint)...........76
    See also Ephrata Brethren
Brumbaugh, Martin. (source, see
    Bibliography).................74
Brumfield, Francis, & Co........127
Brunswick Gazette, New Brunswick,
    N.J...........................239
Bryan, _____ 354, 355
Brynberg & Andrews...............251
Brynberg & Porter................251
Brynberg, Peter.............251, 252
Buchan, Dr. William. Domestic
    Medicine.....................213
Buckner, John..........100, 277, 278
Budd, Thomas................4, 5, 56
_____ . Good Order Established
    in Pennsilvania & New-Jersey...4
Buel & Joyner....................189
Buel & Mitchell..................185
Buel, David......................212
Buel, Jesse...........179-80, 185-86
                  189, 197, 210
Buell, William S.............209, 252
Bullock, Archibald..........378, 381
Bunce & Hobby....................398

Bunce, Josiah.....................214
Bunce, William J..................398
Bunyan, John......................374
Burd & Haswell....................334
Burd & Hughes................334, 394
Burd, John........................335
Burd, Joseph V.........334, 335, 394
Burgess, Samuel...................272
Burgoyne, John....................173
Burkloe & Mears...................359
Burling, Thomas...................128
Burlington Advertiser, Burlington,
    New Jersey....................235
Burnet, _____. (Gov. of ?)....143
Burnyeat, John. An Epistle . . .
    to Friends in Pensilvania......4
Burr, Aaron.......................273
Bushnell, Robert...................87
Butler, _____ 94
Butler & Lambden...................94
Butler, J.B........................94
Butler, Samuel....................374
By the Proprietary of the Province
    of Pensilvania, and Counties
    annexed With the Advice of the
    Council: A Proclamation. (1699,
    against pirates)...............10

Cabinet, Schenectady, N.Y.........209
Cabinet, Georgetown, D.C.......265-66
                            269, 270
Cabots (explorers)................133
Caesar............................374
Caldwell & Sower..................305
Caldwell, Samuel B. T.............305
Calvert, Cecil, 2d Lord Baltimore
                             99-100
Calvert, Charles (Md. Gov.).......110
Cambridge Gazette, Cambridge, N.Y.218
Camden Intelligencer, Camden, S.C.336
Camden Journal, Camden, S.Car.....336
Cameron, Alexander....63, 163-65, 331
Cameron, J. A.....................215
Campbell, Archibald..........388, 390
Campbell, William..................98
Canfield, Russel..................215

Cape-Fear Herald, Wilmington,
    North Carolina................356
Cape-Fear Mercury, Wilmington,
    North Carolina.......349-51, 355
Cape-Fear Recorder, Wilmington,
    North Carolina................356
Car, Anthony......................152
Carey & Harrison..................334
Carey, James........334, 355-56, 395
Carey, Lusius.....................204
Carey's United States Recorder,
    Phila., Pa....................356
Carlisle Gazette, Carlisle, Pa.86-87
Carmen Seculare, by Richard Lewis
                                112
Carolina Centinel, New Bern, N.C.355
Carolina Federal Republican, New
    Bern, North Carolina....354, 355
Carolina Gazette, Charleston, SC.334
Carolina Observer, Fayetteville,
    North Carolina................360
Carpenter, Samuel...................9
Carpenter, William A..............198
Carson, James................234, 335
Carter, George....................303
Carter, James B...................274
Carter, John......................304
Carter, John M....................274
Carteret, Sir George..........221-22
Carvile, Robert...................104
Cary, John D..................130-31
Case of Miss Mary Roche, more
    fairly Related, The, by
    Dr. Thomas Dale.........318, 320
Case of Miss Mary Roche, who was
    inoculated June 28, 1738, The,
    by Dr. James Killpatrick.....318
Catalogue of Books . . . belonging
    to the Library of the two Houses
    of Congress...................272
Catalogue of the Books belonging
    to the New York Society's
    Library.......................156
Catechism, children's, 1693?......138
Catechism, Indian.........131, 133-34
Catechism, James'.............133-34
Catechism, Larger.................208
Cato..............................374

Cato's Moral Distichs Englished in
    Couplets, James Logan, tr........39
Catskill Packet, Catskill, N.Y.......203
Catskill Recorder, Catskill, N.Y.....203
Caveto, pseud. see William Goddard
Center, Asa A......................179
Centinel, and Country Gazette,
    Georgetown, D.C..................262
Centinel of Freedom, Newark, N.J.....236
Centinel of Liberty, and Georgetown
    Advertiser, Georgetown, D.C......258
                                262, 267
Central Gazette, Charlottesville, Va.299
Chambers, John......................145
Champlain, Samuel de.................132
Character and Duty of Minister and
    People, The, by Josiah Smith.....318
Charge to the Grand Jury, A, by
    William Gooch...............280, 282
Charles I..........................99-100
Charles II.............170, 221, 277-278
Charles, Lord Baltimore.............112
Charleston Courier, S. Car..........179
Charleston Evening Gazette, S.C.334, 394
Charleston Evening Post, S. Car......335
Charleston Gazette, S. Car..........331
Charleston Morning Post, S. Car.333, 334
Chattin, _____ 46
Chattin, James......................78
Chesnuthiller Wochenschrift, Der,
    Chestnut Hill, Pa...............82
Chestertown Gazette, Chestertown, Md.131
Chevee, James A.....................199
Child, I. & W. (firm)..........213, 214
Child, Increase................213, 214
Child of Pallas, Baltimore, Md..128, 265
Child, William.................213, 214
Childs & Swaine.............168-169, 242
Childs, Francis....53, 166, 168-169, 242
Childs, F/ rancis_/ & Co.............168
Childs, Nathan.................333, 334
_____ , & Co.....................333
Child's New Spelling Book, The....245-46
Chilton, Mrs.......................120
Chittenden, George.................191
Christiaens, Annetie...............140
_____ . Husband.................140
Christian Repository, Wilmington, De.251

Christian's, Scholar's and Farmer's
    Magazine, Elizabethtown, N.J..239
Chronicle of Liberty, Charleston,
    South Carolina.................333
Churchill & Abbey.................180
Churchill & McGlashan.............180
Churchill, George.................180
Cicero. De Officiis...............187
Circular-Schreiben der Vereinigten
    Reformirten Prediger in Penn-
    sylvanien......................79
Cist & Steiner.................67, 267
Cist, Carl...............67, 269, 271
Cist, Charles, see Carl Cist
Citizen and Countryman's Experienced
    Farrier, The, by J. Markham,
    G. Jefferies, / et.al._/......248
Citizen & Farmer's Almanac........240
City Gazette & Daily Telegraphe,
    Baltimore, Md.................128
City Gazette, Charleston, SC.333, 334
Claremont Gazette, Statesburg,
    South Carolina.................335
Clark, Samuel W...................192
Clark, Zephaniah..................210
Clarkson & Davis..............290, 299
Clarkson, John................290, 299
Clarkson, Matthew. An Address to
    the Citizens of Philadelphia,
    Respecting the Better Govern-
    ment of Youth..................95
Claxton & Babcock.............175, 194
Claxton, Thomas...............175, 194
Clayland & Dobbin.................128
Clayland, Thomas E................128
Claypoole, David C.................59
Clerical Candidates, a Poem, The..271
Clinton Advertiser, Plattsburg,
    New York.......................219
Clinton, DeWitt (N.Y. Gov)........176
Colden, Cadwallader...............143
_____ . (?) Explication of the
    First Causes of the Action in
    Matter.........................149
Cole, John O......................177
Coleman, Daniel...................251
Colerick, Hunter & Beaumont........95
Colerick, John.....................95

Coles, Dennis........................205
Collection of many Christian Exper-
    iences, by Clement Hall..........346
Collection of Psalms and Hymns, A....318
Collection of the Governor's Several
    Speeches, and the Addresses of
    Each House, A.....................115
Collier & Copp.......................183
Collier, Thomas.................183, 211
Collins, Isaac........45, 49, 67, 233-36
Columbia Gazette, Columbia, S. Car...335
Columbia Magazine, Hudson, N.Y.......191
Columbia Republican, Hudson, N.Y.....193
Columbian Advertiser, Alexandria, Va.301
Columbian Chronicle, Georgetown, D.C.
                          258, 262, 300
Columbian Courier, Upton, N.Y...196, 206
Columbian Herald; or, the New Daily
    Advertiser, Charlestown, S.Car...333
Columbian Herald, or the Patriotic
    Courier of North America, Charles-
    town, South, Carolina.......333, 334
Columbian Mercury, Canaan, N.Y.......206
Columbian Mirror, Alexandria, Va..300-01
Columbian Museum & Savannah Adverti-
    ser, Savannah, Ga............395, 397
Columbian Orator, by Caleb Bingham...212
Columbian Repository, Georgetown, DC.272
Colvin, John B..................128, 273
Colvin's Weekly Register, D.C........273
Comet, Perryopolis, Pa................98
Commercial Register, Norfolk, Va.....294
Commonwealth, Pittsburgh, Pa......94, 97
Compact Maritime, by Thomas Paine....271
Comstock, James......................214
Conditions for New Planters In the
    Territories of His Royal High-
    ness the Duke of York, by Gov.
    Nicolls...........................133
Coney, Rev. Peregrine................104
Confessions . . . , by J. Lackington.217
Congreve, William....................374
Connecticut Gazette, New Haven, Conn.
                      45, 150, 160, 227
Connoly, Lewis.......................360
Connoly, Thomas......................360
Conrad, _____ 95
Conrad, John, & Co...................272

Conrad, Michael & John & Co.......272
Considerations on the Executive Gov-
    ernment of the United States, by
    Augustus B. Woodward..........219
Considerations on the Government of
    the Territory of Columbia, by
    Augustus B. Woodward..........270
Considerations on the Substance of
    the Sun, by Augustus B. Woodward
                                  271
Constable, Daniel.................335
Constitution of the State of
    Georgia, The.............383, 397
Constitutional Courant, Woodbridge,
    New Jersey.................22, 227
Constitutional Diary, Phila., Pa..356
Constitutional Gazette, NYC.......152
Continental Congress...54, 57, 59, 64
    84, 86, 122, 125, 254, 380, 381, 390
    _____. Journals, proceedings and
    votes, printed........59, 84, 173
    _____. see also U.S. Congress
Coode, Colonel John. The Declara-
    tion of the Reasons and Mo-
    tives for the Present Appear-
    ing in Arms of their Majest-
    ies Protestant Subjects in the
    Province of Maryland..........101
Cooke, Ebenezer.............112, 114
    _____. The Sot-Weed Factor; or
    a Voyage to Maryland..........114
    _____. The Sotweed Redivivus...114
Cooper & Russell.................240
Cooper, Elijah...................240
Cooper, Ezekiel..................217
Cooper, W. D. History of North
    America......................196
Cooper, William..................273
Cooper, William. The Promised Seed
                                  214
Copp & Freer.....................185
Copp, William................183, 185
Copson, John......................14
Coram, Robert....................251
Cornwallis, Lord............331, 391
Corss, Richard L..........192-93, 203
Cosby, William (N.Y. Gov)......142-46
Cossart, Theophilus...............80

Cossens, _____ 322
Coulter, James......................78
Country Journal, and the Poughkeepsie
    Advertiser, Poughkeepsie, N.Y..186
Coupee & Slump....................361
Coupee, Francis...................361
Courier, Fredericksburg, Va.......303
Courier de l'Amerique, Phila., Pa...67
Courtney, John....................304
Cowan, James......................130
Cowper, John......................294
Cox & Sheppard...................334
Cox, Thomas Campbell.............334
Craft & Black...................235-36
Craft, Gershom....................235
Craig, Frederick................250-51
_____, & Co....................250
Cramer & Spear...................93-94
Cramer, Elizabeth..................94
Cramer, Spear & Eichbaum.........93-94
Cramer, Susan......................94
Cramer, Zadok....................92-94
Crawford, Duglad. Searmoin chuaidh
    a liobhairt aig an Raft-Swamp..360
Crawford Weekly Messenger, Meadville,
    Pennsylvania....................97
Cree, David.......................240
Crocker, John, & Co...........260, 264
Crossfield, Jehiel................273
Croswell & Frary................191-93
Croswell, Harry..........191-94, 203
Croswell, Mackay..................203
_____, & Co....................203
Croswell, T. & M..................204
Crouch, Charles....322, 324, 331, 350?
Crouch, Mary Wilkinson.............331
Crowell, Timothy B............198, 205
Crukshank & Collins...............234
Crukshank, Joseph.........22, 67, 234
Culpeper, Lord Thomas (Va. Gov.)276-77
Cumming, _____ 293
Cunningham, John..................220
Curtis, Daniel....................197
Curtis, Daniel, Jr................210

Daggett, Herman. American Reader.187
Daily Advertiser, NYC.....166, 168-69
Daily Advertiser, Phila., Pa......356
Daily Evening Gazette and Charles-
    ton Tea-Table Companion, S.Car.334
Daily Intelligencer, Baltimore,
    Maryland......................126
Daily Repository, Baltimore, Md.126-7
Dale, Dr. Thomas..................318
_____. The Case of Miss Mary
    Roche, more fairly related.318-20
Daniell, William...................47
Daveiss, Joseph H.................273
Davie, William Richardson. Instruc-
    tions to be Observed for the
    Formations and Movements of the
    Cavalry.......................358
Davis & Pleasants.................300
Davis, Augustine...290, 297, 299, 300
Davis, James.......291, 338, 340, 342
                  344, 346, 348, 351-52
Davis, James Jr...................346
Davis, John.......................304
Davis, John.......................346
Davis, Joseph.....................333
Davis, Matthew L..................242
Davis, Thomas.342, 346, 348, 356, 358
Davis, William...............294, 302
Davis, William....................346
Davison, Gideon M.................220
Davison, William..................294
Day, Ambrose......................398
Day & Hancock................256, 258
Day & Hely........................398
Day & Hopkins.....................235
Day, M.......................256, 258
Day, Matthias & Co................235
Dealers Pocket Companion..........280
Debates and other Proceedings of the
    Convention of Virginia, Convened
    at Richmond . . . 1788, for the
    purpose of deliberating on the
    Constitution recommended by the
    Grand Federal Convention......302
Debrahm, William..................272
Declaration of Independence
                      54, 57, 117
Declaration of Rights.............123

Declaration of Rights and Constitution
made by the Halifax Convention
in December, 1776 (N.Car.).....359
Declaration of the Reasons . . . for
the Present Appearing in Arms of
. . . Subjects in . . . /Md./..101
Defoe, Daniel.................156, 374
DeForest, Henry.......140-41, 150, 152
Delancey, James............142, 145-46
Delaware & Eastern-Shore Advertiser,
    Wilmington, Delaware........250-51
Delaware Courant, Wilmington, Del..250
Delaware Freeman, Wilmington, Del..252
Delaware Gazette, Wilmington, Del-
    aware..................250, 251, 252
Delaware Gazette (2d), Wilmington,
    Delaware........................252
Delaware Gazette (3d), Wilmington,
    Delaware........................252
Delaware Patriot, Wilmington, Del..252
Delaware State Journal, Wilmington,
    Delaware...................251, 252
Delaware state printing........37, 246
                              268, 252
Delaware Statesman, Wilmington, De.252
Dellawaerische Gesang-Büchlein, by
    Bernhard Adam Grubé.............82
Democratic Republican, Baltimore,
    Maryland........................128
Denham, _____ 27-28
Denman, M. M......................240
Denniston, David..................204
Denton & Hopkins..................198
Denton, Gabriel...................198
De Officiis, by Cicero............187
Deputy Commissary's Guide, by Elie
    Vallette........................116
Dering, Henry P...................202
Detection of the Conduct and Proceed-
    ings . . . at the Oxford Meeting
    House . . . A...................118
Deutsche Porcupein, Der, Lancaster,
    Pennsylvania....................80
Devoran, Catherine.................105
Devoran, Dinah (Nuthead)...........105
Devoran, Manus.....................105
Dialogue Between and /sic / Subscri-
    ber and a Nonsubscriber........315

Dialogue between Thomas Sweet-Scented,
    . . . and Justice Love-Country,
    . . . , by William Gooch.......282
Diary, New York, N.Y..............162
Dickinson, John. "Letters from a
    Farmer"...................23, ?148
Dickinson, Jonathan. Gods Protecting
    Providence 10
Dictionary of the English Language,
    A, by Samuel Johnson..........374
Dictionary of the Holy Bible, by
    John Brown..................92-93
Dillworth, _____ . Spelling Book..95
Dinmore & Cooper..................273
Dinmore, Richard..........266-67, 272
                          273, 301-2
_____, comp. Select and Fugitive
    Poetry..................267, 272
Discourse Concerning the Faith, A..262
Discovery, Settlement and present
    State of Kentucke, by John
    Filson........................248
Disseminator (proposed) Catskill,
    New York......................203
Dissertations on the Prophesies, by
    Bishop Thomas Newton..........239
Dixon & Holt......................299
Dixon & Hunter....................290
Dixon & Meriwether................299
Dixon & Nicolson.........290, 295, 297
Dixon, John..............288, 290, 295
                         297, 299, 300
Dixon, John Jr....................299
Dobbin, Thomas....................128
Dobbs, _____ (N.Car. Gov.).342, 344
                              348, 349
Dodd & Rumsey.....................207
Dodd & Stevenson............207, 240
Dodd, Edward......................207
Dodd, Henry.......................207
Dodd, Henry W.....................207
Dodd, Rumsey & Stevenson..........207
Doddridge, Phillip. Plain and Seri-
    ous Address to the Master of a
    Family on the Importance of Fam-
    ily Religion..................200
Dodge & Pennington................236
Dodge, Daniel.....................236

Domestic Medicine, by Dr. William
   Buchan........................213
Dongan, Thomas (NY Gov.)..........134
Donkin, Major. Military Collections
   and Remarks...................159
Doubleday, U. F..............180, 214
Douglas, Charles..................200
Douglas, Nathan...................189
Douglass, _____...............240
Douglass, David...................329
Doyle, Alexander.............256, 258
Doyle, James.................256, 258
Dromgoole & Engledow..............305
Drucks der Bruederschafft..........77
   see also Ephrata Brethren
Dryden, John......................374
Duane, William...........269-70, 272
Duane, William, & Son.......270, 272
Dulheuer, Henry...................126
Duncan, William...................292
Duncan, William, & Co.............292
Dunkers, see Ephrata Brethren
Dunlap & Claypoole...........59, 363
Dunlap & Hayes...........125, 297-99
Dunlap, John.......57, 59-60, 62, 79
     80, 84, 118-19, 125, 297-99
Dunlap, William....46, 57, 64, 66,79
             125, 168
Dunlap's Maryland Gazette, Balti-
   more, Maryland...........84, 297
Dunmore, Lord................161, 292
Durell, William...................215
Dutch East India Company.........132
Dutch West India Company.........132
Dutchess Observer, Poughkeepsie,
   New York......................190
Duyckinck, E......................204
Dyche, _____. untitled spelling
   book..........................346

Eagle of Freedom, Baltimore,
   Maryland......................128
Eagle, or, Carlisle Herald,
   Carlisle, Penna................87
Eakly, John.........................6

East-Florida Gazette. St. Augustine,
   Florida.......................329
Eaton, Edward. Almanac for 1688......5
Eckerlin, Israel...................77
Eddy, George Simpson. Account Books
   Kept by Benjamin Franklin (1728-
   1747)..........................52
Edenton Gazette, Edenton, N.Car....361
Edenton Gazette (2d) Edenton,
   North Carolina................361
Edenton Intelligencer, Edenton,
   North Carolina................360
Edie & M'Clellan...................86
Edie, James........................86
Edie, John.........................86
Edwards, Philip..............127, 251
Ehrliche Kurtzweiliche Deutsche
   Americanische Geschichts und
   Haus Calender, auf das jar
   . . . 1764.................80, 82
Eichbaum & Johnston................94
Eichbaum, William Jr.............93-94
Elderkin & Miller.................235
Elegy On the much Lamented Death of
   the Ingenious and Well-Beloved
   Aquila Rose, Clerk to the Hon-
   ourable Assembly at Philadelphia,
   who died the 24th of the 4th
   month, 1723, Aged 28, An, by
   Samuel Keimer.................17
Eliot's Indian Bible...............70
Elizabeth Daily Journal, Elizabeth,
   New Jersey....................237
Elliott, _____.................88
Elliot & Burd.....................335
Elliot & Stiles....................57
Elliot, James......................57
Elliot, Nathan..............194, 203
Elliott, Jonathan.................275
Elliott, William.................275
Elliston, Robert. Enchiridium Poly-
   chrestum......................149
Enchiridium Polychrestum, by Robert
   Elliston......................149
Encyclopedian Instructor, Edenton,
   North Carolina................361
Engledow, Robert..................305

Engles, Silas........................94
English, David..258, 262, 265, 269-71
English Grammar, Wrote in a Plain
    Familiar Manner.................44
Enquiries into the Necessity . . .
    of . . . Legislation over the
    District of Columbia..........270
Epaminondas, pseud. see Augustus
    B. Woodward
Epaminondas on the Government of
    the Territory of Columbia, by
    Augustus B. Woodward..........270
Ephrata Brethren........69, 70, 75-78
Ephrata Press, ...70, 76-77
Epistle from John Burnyeat to
    Friends in Pensilvania..........4
Epistle from the Yearly Meeting....13
"Epistle to Friends to be read in
    their Monthly Meeting," by
    Frances Taylor...................4
Erfahrene Americanische Haus-unt
    Stall-Arzt, Der...............129
Erskine, Rev. Ralph. The Harmony
    of Divine Attributes..........218
Essay on Currency, Written in
    August, 1732, An.........308, 316
Essay on Infant Baptism...........208
Essex Patriot, Elizabethtown, N.Y.220
Eulogy on George Washington, by
    Francis Kinloch...............335
Evangelien-Harmonie, in die Delaware
    Sprache Übersetzt. Bernhard
    Adam Grube, translator.........82
Evans, Charles. American Biblio-
    graphy..............78, 173, 245
Evans, John J.....................334
Evening Courier, Charleston,
    South Carolina................334
Evening Post & General Advertiser,
    Charleston, South Carolina.334-35
Evitt, William.....................67
Ewen, _____ 367
Ewing, _____ 88
Examination of the Reverend John
    Anderson's Discourse on the
    Divine Ordinance of Singing
    Psalms, by John Black..........86
Examinations of Dr. Benjamin

Franklin, before an August Assem-
    bly, relating to the Repeal of
    the Stamp Act.................291
Examiner, Richmond, Virginia......299
Explication of the First Causes of
    Action in Matter, by Cadwallader
    Colden........................149
"Expostulations of Potowmac, The"
                                256-58

Fahnestock, Conrad.................83
Fairfax, Bryan. Strictures on the
    Second Part of the Age of Reason
                                  262
Falkner, William...............244-46
Farley, Samuel....................152
Farmer, Poughkeepsie, New York....205
Farmer's Journal & Newton Advertiser,
    Newton, New Jersey........198, 243
"Farmer's Letters"............23?, 148
Farmer's Oracle & Lansingburgh Weekly
    Gazette, Lansingburgh, N.Y.
                             197, 210
    moved to Troy, New York...197, 210
Farmers' Register, Greensburg, Pa...97
Farmers' Register, Lansingburgh,
    New York..................197, 211
    moved to Troy, New York........211
Farmer's Register, Kingston, New
    York......................183, 185
Faust, Daniel.....................335
Faust, Jacob J....................335
Fauteux, Aegidius. The Introduction
    of Printing into Canada.........64
Fayette Gazette, Uniontown, Pa......97
Fayetteville Gazette, Fayetteville,
    No. Car.........302, 355, 359, 360
Fayetteville Gazette (2d) Fayette-
    ville, North Carolina.........359
Federal Ark, The, Wilmington,
    Delaware..................252, 253
    from Dover, Delaware......252, 253
Federal Carolina Gazette, Charleston,
    South Carolina............327, 335
Federal Gazette and Baltimore Daily
    Advertiser, Baltimore, Md......127

Federal Herald, Albany, N.Y..175, 194
    moved to Lansingburgh, N.Y.
                            175, 194-96
Federal Intelligencer, Baltimore,
    Maryland......................126
Federal Post, Trenton, N.J........235
Federal Republican, Baltimore, Md.274
    moved to Georgetown, D.C......275
Federalist, Trenton, N.J..........225
Fee, Robert.......................97
Fellows, J.......................204
Ferguson, Robert..............94, 358
Field, _____ 303
Field, Thomas................302, 303
Fielding, Henry...................374
Fierer & Fosdick...........256, 303-4
Fierer, Charles....255-56, 258, 303-4
Filson, John. The Discovery, Settle-
    ment and present State of
    Kentucke, by John Filson.....248
Fincastle Weekly Advertiser,
    Fincastle, Virginia...........305
Findlay, Jonathan Smith...265, 273-74
Flagg, Azariah C..................219
Fleeming, _____ 163
Fletcher, Benjamin (Gov. of Penna.
    and N.Y.)...8-9, 135-38, 140, 172
Forward, Walter....................92
Fosdick, Thomas U..........256, 303-4
Foster, William....................92
Four Discourses on the General Prin-
    ciples of Deism and Revelation
    Contrasted, by Samuel Eusebius
    McCorkle......................361
Fowle, Zachariah..................349
Fowler, William...................301
Fox, _____ 149
Fox, George.........................1
Fox, James..........................9
Fox, Justus...................75, 127
Frame of the Government of the
    Province of Pennsilvania and
    Territories there-unto annexed,
    in America, The.................6
Frankfurter Landkompagnie..........68
Franklin, _____ 354
Franklin & Armbruster..........33, 48
Franklin & Bohm................33, 48

Franklin & Garrow.................354
Franklin & Hall........22, 33, 36, 49
                            244-45, 248
Franklin & Holland.................47
Franklin & Mecom...................44
Franklin & Meredith.......310, 328-29
                                332, 339
Franklin & Parker...........44, 49-52
Franklin & Timothy.........41-42, 315
Franklin & Whitmarsh.........41, 313
Franklin, Benjamin...16-24, 25-55, 57
    64, 68, 77-79, 84, 115, 121, 122
  140, 152, 168, 227, 229, 231-33, 244
    284, 291, 310, 314, 315, 318, 320
                            322, 324, 325
_____ . Autobiography....20, 29, 32
                        34-35, 39, 41-42
_____ . A Modest Enquiry into the
    Nature and Necessity of a Paper-
    Currency.....................28-29
_____ . The Way to Wealth.......194
_____ . will...................53-54
Franklin, Deborah (Read)........22-23
                            26, 46, 233
Franklin, James...25, 27, 30, 44, 318
_____ . widow....................44
Franklin, James Jr.................44
Franklin, Josiah................26-27
Franklin, William (N.J. Gov.).22, 231
Franklinian Library, see Setauket.
Frary, Jonathan...................191
Frederick-Town Herald, Frederick-
    town, Maryland.................87
Freedom of the press...6, 8, 32, 108
        122, 123, 124, 134, 135, 141
    146, 148-49, 154, 276-78, 290, 325
    see also John Peter Zenger
Freeman & Andrews.................178
Freeman, Edward...................178
Freemason's Monitor, Albany, N.Y.180
Freer, Anthony....................185
Freer, S. & A. (firm).............185
Freer, Samuel.....................185
Freer, Samuel, & Sons.............185
Freer, Samuel S...................185
Freiheitsvogel, Sunbury, Penna....83
French, Colonel....................26
Freneau & Davis...................242

Freneau & Minut....................242
Freneau, Philip.........156, 158, 159
                              169, 242
_____. "Petition /of Hugh
   Gaine/"...................156, 158
   . Poems....................242
Fresh Advices from Canada.........173
Friend of the People, Richmond,Va.301
Frothingham, David............199-200
Frothingham's Long Island Herald,
   Sag Harbor, L.I., N.Y.....199-200
Fry, Joseph.......................178
Full and Clear Reply to Doct.
   Thomas Dale, A, by Dr. James
   Killpatrick...................322
Full and Impartial View of Mr.
   Bowman's Visitation Sermon,A..315
Fulton, John......................386

Gaiatonsera ionteweienstakwa, ongwe
   onwe gawennontakon, by Eleazer
   Williams. (Iroquois spelling
   book)..........................219
Gaine, Hugh...152, 154, 156, 158, 159
                              161, 236
Gales & Seaton....................268
Gales, Joseph.................66, 363
Gales, Joseph Jr.............268, 363
Gales's Independent Gazetteer,
   Philadelphia, Pennsylvania....363
Galloway, Joseph........23-24, 61, 66
Gambler, or Memoirs of a British
   Officer, The...................272
Gardner & Billings................210
Gardner & Hill...............196, 210
Gardner, George.........196, 206, 210
Garrow, ...354
Gates, Horatio.....................86
Gazette, unnamed, Savannah,
   Georgia........383, 385, 386, 388
Gazette de Montreal, Quebec........64
Gazette de Quebec, Quebec......64, 66
Gazette du Commerce et Litteraire,
   La, Montreal, Quebec...........64
Gazette of the State of Georgia,
   Savannah, Georgia.............393

Gazette of the State of South
   Carolina, Charleston, S.Car....326
Gazette Publications, by Hugh Henry
   Brackenridge....................90
Gazlay, Ward M....................205
Geistliches Magazien, Ein,
   Germantown, Pennsylvania........75
Gemeinützige Philadelphische Corres-
   pondenz, Philadelphia, Penna....67
General Epitsle Given forth by the
   People of the Lord, called,
   Quakers.........................4
General Geography, and Rudiments of
   Useful Knowledge, by H. G.
   Spafford.......................193
General Magazine, And Historical
   Chronicle, For all the British
   Plantations in America, Phila-
   delphia, Pennsylvania....16, 38-39
General Post-Bothe, Philadelphia,
   Pennsylvania....................67
General Staatsbote, Der, Frederick,
   Maryland.................129, 130
Genius of Liberty, Fredericksburg,
   Virginia......................303
Genius of Liberty, Leesburg, Va....305
Genius of Liberty, Morristown, N.J.240
Genius of Liberty, New Brunswick,
   New Jersey....................239
Genius of Liberty, Uniontown, Pa....97
Gentleman's Pocket Farrier, by
   Henry Bracken............95, 318
Gentleman's Political Almanac for
   1796..........................301
George II................142, 308, 325
Georgetown Chronicle, Georgetown,
   South Carolina.................335
Georgetown Gazette, Georgetown,
   South Carolina.................335
Georgetown Museum, Georgetown, D.C.
                        262, 265, 269
George-town Weekly Ledger, Georgetown,
   District of Columbia......256, 258
Georgia Act of Attainder (1st).....381
                              383, 385
Georgia Act of Amercement.........392
Georgia Act of Attainder (1st).....381
                              383, 385
Georgia Act of Attainder (2d).391, 392

380-81, 383, 385-88. 391-94, 397
Georgia Assembly. House. Journal
                              375, 397
Georgia Constitution.......383, 397
Georgia Gazette, Savannah, Ga....370
     372, 374-76, 378, 380-81, 383
Georgia Gazette, Savannah, Ga....383
                              386, 388
Georgia Gazette, Savannah, Ga.394-95
                              397-99
Georgia Governor
     John Reynolds.................366
     John Adam Treutlen............381
     James Wright....367-68, 370, 372
                    378, 380, 390, 392
Georgia Journal and Independent
     Federal Register, Savannah,
     Georgia.................356, 395
Georgia laws, acts of assembly, etc.
     366-68, 370, 372, 374, 376, 381
     383, 385, 387, 391, 392, 394
                              397
Georgia State Gazette, or Indepen-
     dent Register, Augusta, Ga...394
Georgia state printing...........383
German Baptists see Ephrata
     Brethren
Germantowner Zeitung, Germantown,
     Pennsylvania...................75
Gerrisch, Georg or George D.
     Gerrish........82-83, 131, 206-7
Gesangdereinsamen und Verlassenen
     Turtel-Taube Nemlich der Christ-
     lichen Kirche, Das...........77
Gibson, James B..................207
Gignilliat, Henry................314
Gilkinson, John...................92
Gilleland, James C...............94
Gilmore, Thomas...............64, 66
Gilmour, Robert..................292
Gilpin, Thomas...................252
Gird, Henry Jr.................300-1
Glebe House, The, by a Lady of
     Distinction...................243
Glen, James (S. Car. Gov.).......322
Goddard & Oswald...............123-4
Goddard, Dr. Giles...............121
Goddard, Mary Katherine..120, 122-25

Goddard, Sarah....................22
Goddard, William.22-24, 45, 61, 66-67
                118, 119, 120-27, 229
                              233, 236
_____. The Prowess of the Whig
     Club..........................123
Gods Protecting Providence Man's
     Surest Help . . . , by Jonathan
     Dickinson.....................10
Gomez, Benjamin..............215, 217
Gooch, William (Va. Gov.).........282
_____. A Charge to the Grand
     Jury....................280, 282
_____. A Dialogue between
     Thomas Sweet-Scented, William
     Oronoco, Planters, both Men of
     good Understanding, and Justice
     Love-Country, who can speak for
     himself.......................282

Good Order Established in Pennsil-
     vania & New-Jersey in America,
     Being a true Account of the
     Country; With its Produce and
     Commodities there made..........4
Goodenow, Sterling...............211
Goodwin, George..............173, 175
Goshen Repository & Weekly Intelli-
     gencer, Goshen, N.Y............198
Graham, David....................126
Grant & Wells....................218
Greek grammar, by Barclay.........374
Green & English....258, 262, 264, 265
                         269, 270, 271
Green & Rind.................116, 291
Green, Anne Catherine (Hoof)...115-17
Green, Charles D...258, 262, 265, 269
                              270, 271
Green, English & Co..............262
Green family.........1, 115, 116, 117
Green, Frederick.................117
Green, Jonas.........114-16, 117, 291
Green, Jonas.....................117
Green, Mary (Flint)..............115
Green, Robert....................388
Green, Samuel..........115, 117, 133
Green, Samuel...............117, 200
Green, Thomas................45, 150

Green, Timothy "Deacon"..........115
Green, Timothy....................115
Green Timothy IV..................302
Green, William....................117
Greene & Delaware Washingtonian,
    Catskill, N.Y........192-93, 203
Greenleaf, Ann....................162
Greenleaf, Thomas.................162
Greenleaf's New-York, Connecticut &
    New Jersey Almanack or Diary.215
Greenman, Joseph G................203
Grieves, Phebe (Herbert).........131
Grieves, Thomas...................131
Groff, _____ 268-69
Growden, Joseph.....................6
Grubé, Bernhard Adam...............82
_____ , tr. Evangelen-Harmonie
    in die Delaware Sprache ü
    bersetzt.......................82
_____ , tr. Dellawaerische
    Gesang-Büchlein...............82
Gruber, Johann..............130, 131
Guardian, Poughkeepsie, New York.189
Guardian, New Brunswick, N.J.....239
Guide to Vestrymen...............149
Gwynn, William...............76, 127

Haff, _____ 303
Hall, Allmand...............354, 356
Hall & Bryan...............354, 355
Hall & Pierie.....................57
Hall & Sellers........50, 57, 60, 86
Hall, Clement. A Collection of
    many Christian Experiences...346
Hall, David...........22, 33, 46-47
                    49-50, 54, 57
_____ , sons....................50
Hall, David, Jr...........57, 84, 86
Hall, Edmund...............112, 279
Hall, Joseph......................88
Hall, Dr. Lyman..................381
Hall, Salmon..................354-56
Hall, William....................119
Hall, William.........57, 84, 86
Hall, William, Jr.................57
Hall's Wilmington Gazette, Wilming-
    ton, North Carolina.........356

Halland, Henry....................192
Hamilton, _____ 74
Hamilton, Alexander..........163, 237
_____ . Letters from Phocion....163
Hamilton, Andrew.........145-46, 148
Hamilton, James....................33
Hamilton, William..................80
Hammerer, John Daniel.............388
Hancock, W..................256, 258
Handshuh, Rev. Johann Friederich...34
Hanna, _____ 128
Hanson, Alexander C..............275
Hanson & Bond.............258, 300
Hanson & Briggs..................258
Hanson & Priestley...............258
Hanson, Captain _____ 350
Hanson, Samuel..........258, 262, 300
Harison, _____ (Gov. of ?).....143
Harmer & Isler...................303
Harmer, Joseph...................303
Harmony of the Divine Attributes,
    The, by Rev. Ralph Erskine....218
Harrisburger Morgenröthe, Harrisburg,
    Pennsylvania...................83
Harrison, Francis................144
Harrison, William Primrose...333, 334
Harrison, William Primrose, & Co..333
Harry, David..................21, 24
Hasselbach, Catherine............118
Hasselbach, Nicholas..........22, 48
                    80, 118, 120
Haswell, Robert..................334
Hawkins, Joseph. History of a Voy-
    age to the Coast of Africa....212
Hayes & Killen..........125, 126, 250
Hayes, James Jr..........125, 297-99
Hayes, John..............125-26, 250
Heartt, Dennis...................358
Hedges, Jesse....................200
Heiskell, William................303
Hely, James......................398
Henkel, Ambrosus.................305
Herald, Connellsville, Penna.......98
Herald of Freedom, Edenton, North
    Carolina..................354, 361
Herald of Freedom and the Federal
    Advertiser, Boston, Mass......178
Herald of Liberty, Washington,
    Pennsylvania..........92, 95, 97

Herald of Virginia, Fincastle,
    Virginia......................305
Herbert, Phebe....................131
Herbert, Stewart............79, 130-31
Heron, _____ 198
Herrington, Jacob..................98
Hewes, John.......................127
Hewet, _____ 104
Hickock, _____ 194
Hicks, John..................163, 165
High-Dutch and English Gazette,
    Philadelphia, Penna.....33, 47-48
Hildeburn, Charles R. (source, see
    Bibliography).........48, 78, 245
Hill, Ebenezer....................210
Hill, James.............196, 206, 210
Hillsborough Recorder, Hillsborough,
    North Carolina................358
Hinchman, Robert................204-5
History of a Voyage to the Coast
    of Africa, by Joseph Hawkins..212
History of Colonel Nathaniel
    Bacon's Rebellion in Virginia.
    Done into Hudibrastick Verse,
    from an old Ms, The...........114
History of New Jersey, by _____
    Smith..........................45
History of North America, by
    W. D. Cooper..................196
History of the Colony of Nova-Cae-
    saria or New-Jersey, by Samuel
    Smith..............229, 231, 232
History of the Life and Death
    . . . of General George Wash-
    ington, by Rev. Mason L.
    Weems..............239, 262, 264
History of the Revolution of South
    Carolina, by David Ramsay.....235
History of the Rise, Increase, and
    Progress, Of the Christian
    People called Quakers, The, by
    William Sewel..........17-19, 28
Hive, or Repository of Literature,
    Washington, D.C...............274
Hobby, W. J.......................398
Hoch-Deutsch Americanische Calender,
    Der............................70

Hoch-Deutsch Pennsylvanische Gesch-
    icht-Schreiber, Germantown, Pa.70
Hoch Teutsche und Englische Zeitung,
    or The High-Dutch and English
    Gazette, Philadelphia, Penna.
                      33, 47, 48, 79
Hodge, Abraham........352, 354, 356
                      358-61, 363
Hodge & Blanchard............352, 359
Hodge & Boylan..........354, 360, 363
Hodge & Shober............118-19, 152
Hodge & Wills........352, 356, 358-60
Hodge, Robert............118-20, 152
Hodge's North Carolina Almanac....358
Holdsworth, Edward. Muscipula, sive
    Kambpomyomaxia................112
Holland, Samuel.........46-47, 78-79
Hollingshead, William.............356
Holmes, Capt......................26
Holston Intelligencer, Abingdon,
    Virginia......................305
Holt & Parker......................22
Holt, Charles................192, 193
Holt, Elizabeth....................66
Holt, Elizabeth................161-62
Holt, John.......22, 66, 121, 123,150
            159, 160-61, 183, 186, 284
Holt, John Hunter....161, 292-93, 299
Homespun, Henry, Jr. pseud., see
    Solomon Southwick, Jr.
Honeywood, St. John........196, 206-7
Hood, John B......................336
Hopkins & Heron...................198
Hopkins & Hurtin..................243
Hopkins, Eliot...............198, 243
Hopkins, Francis. A Pretty Story
    Written in the Year of our
    Lord 2774 /sic /..............291
Hopkins, George F............235, 239
Horace............................374
Horner, Samuel........63, 163, 165-66
Hosford, E. & E...................180
Hosford, Elijah...................180
Hosford, Elisha...................180
Hoskins, Timothy.............207, 220
Houghton, A. O..............198, 205
Houghton, T. L....................198

Houstoun, John..............378, 381
Howard & Roulstone..........359, 360
Howard, Caleb D..........355, 359-60
Howard, Lord Francis of Effingham.
  (Va. Gov.)............100, 277-78
Howard, Martin......................349
Howe & Brown..................213-14
Howe, John.................... 213-4
Howe, Lord.................158-59, 181
Howell, Benoni H...................205
Hubbard, John. American Reader...212
Hudson & Goodwin............173, 175
Hudson, Barzillai.................173
Hudson, Henry.....................132
Hudson Weekly Gazette, Hudson, New
  York...................175, 190-91
Hughes, _____ 46
Hughes, Edward....................324
Hughes, Greenberry (Greenbury)
                        334, 394
"humble Confession, Declaration,
  Recantation and Apology of Ben-
  jamin Towne, The," by Dr. Jona-
  than Witherspoon................62
Hume, David.......................374
Humphrey, Constance H. "Check-List
  of New Jersey Imprints . . ."
  (see Bibliography)............232
Humphreys, Daniel..................66
Humphreys, James, Jr........60-61, 62
Humphreys, James, Sr..........60-61
Humphreys, James, Sr. sons.........61
Hunter, Miles.....................302
Hunter, Robert (Gov. of ?)........143
Hunter, William.....95, 284, 286, 288
Hunter, William, Jr..........288, 290
Hurtin & Denton...................198
Hurtin, John G....................198
Hurtin, William.............198, 243
Hütter, Christian Jacob............80

Impartial Gazette, Mt. Pleasant,
  New York.......................215
Impartial Journal, Leesburg, Va...305

Impartial Narrative of . . . the
  Irish Rebellion 1798, by John
  Jones..........................218
Impartial Observer, & Washington
  Advertiser, Washington, D.C.
                  260, 264, 268
Impartial View of the . . . Contro-
  versy between the . . . Federal-
  ists and Republicans.........271
Independent American, Ballston
  Spa, New York.............213, 214
Independent American, Georgetown,
  District of Columbia...........274
Independent Citizen, or, the Majesty
  of the People Asserted against
  the Usurpation of the Legisla-
  ture of North-Carolina.....351-52
Independent Gazetteer, Philadelphia
  Pennsylvania.........66, 124, 162
Independent Journal: or, the General
  Advertiser, NYC, NY...174, 293-94
Independent Ledger, Petersburg,
  Virginia..................294, 302
Independent New-York Gazette, New
  York, New York...........161, 186
Independent Reflector, New York,
  N.Y............................154
Independent Register, Winchester,
  Virginia.......................303
Independent Republican, Montgomery,
  New York.......................199
  moved to Goshen, N.Y..........199
Indian Bible.......................70
Indian catechism (unprinted)......131
         (another)............133-34
Inslee & Car......................152
Inslee, Samuel....................152
Instructor, New York, N.Y.........150
Interesting Life Travels, Voyages
  and Daring Engagements of the
  Celebrated Paul Jones.........194
Invitation to Emigrate to the
  Western Country, An...........130
Iredell, James....................352
Isler, Peter......................303
Israel, John...........92, 93, 95, 97

Jacacks, Nicholas..................190
Jackson, Christopher..............128
Jackson, Major William. Oration....88
Jamaica Assembly....................47
    its printing....................47
Jamaica Courant, Kingston, Jamaica.47
Jamaica Mercury, Kingston, Jam....329
James, Duke of York.....133, 134, 221
James II..........................100
James, Rev. Thomas................133
Jansen, Joseph, see Joseph Reyners
Jansen, Reinier (or Reynier).....9-13
Jansen, Tiberius, see Tiberius
    Johnson
Jefferson, Thomas..116, 213, 267, 269
                272, 290, 297-98
_____. Manual of Parliamentary
    Practice.......................271
Jenings, Samuel. Truth Rescued from
    Forgery & Falshood . . . /sic/.10
Jennings, Samuel..................137
Jersey Chronicle, Mt. Pleasant,
    New Jersey.....................242
John Englishman, New York, N.Y....150
Johnson & Preston.................252
Johnson, Benjamin..................82
Johnson, Guy. Manual Exercise . . .
    to be observed . . . by the
    militia of the Province of
    New York.......................172
Johnson, Joseph...................252
Johnson, Peter A..................240
Johnson, Robert (S. Car. Gov.)....308
                312-13, 314
Johnson, Samuel. A Dictionary of
    the English Language..........374
Johnson, T........................209
Johnson, Tiberius................10-13
Johnson, Sir William....163, 170, 172
Johnston, _____ (N. Car. Gov.)
                337-38
Johnston & Stockton................94
Johnston, James....368, 370-76, 380-1
    383, 385, 388, 390-95, 397, 398-99
Johnston, James (father).....370, 399
Johnston, James & Nicholas (firm)
                394-95, 397, 398
Johnston, Jean Nisbet.............399

Johnston, Lewis...................390
Johnston, Nicholas......394, 395, 397
                398-99
Johnston, Nicholas, & Co.....397, 399
Johnston, Samuel R.................94
Johnston, Sarah Lawrence.....375, 392
                394, 399
Jones, Evan..................107, 108
Jones, John.........................9
Jones, John. Impartial Narrative of
    . . . the Irish Rebellion......218
Jones, Joseph.....................252
Jones, Meriwether............294, 299
Jones, Noble Wymberley.......378, 381
Jones Paul, The Interesting Life,
    travels, Voyages & Daring
    Engagements of the Celebrated.194
Jones, Samuel. The Most Important
    Question, What is Truth.......278
Josephus..........................374
Journal of the Proceedings in the
    Detection of the Conspiracy
    Formed by Some White People
    . . . , A.....................149
Joutard, Valantin..................64
Joyner, Nathaniel.................189
Jungman, Gottlob..........82-83, 130
Justice and Policy of Taxing the
    American Colonies, In Great
    Britain, Considered, by
    Maurice Moore.................349

Kalendarium Pennsilvaniense, or,
    America's Messenger. Being an
    Almanack For the Year of Grace,
    1686.............................2
Kammerer, Heinrich.................67
Kammerer, Heinrich, Jr............235
Keach, Benjamin. The Travels of
    True Godliness & Ungodliness..208
Keimer, Samuel.....16-21, 26-30,   37
                138, 227, 310
_____. An Elegy on the . . .
    Death of . . . Aquila Rose . . 17
Keith, George.......7-8, 56, 136, 138
_____. An Appeal from the Twenty-

eight Judges 8, 136
_____ . The Power of the Gospel
in the Conversion of Sinners.107
_____ . Truth Advanced in the
Correction of many Gross
and hurtful Errors 138
Keith, Robert 348, 351
Keith, Sir William (Penna. Gov.)26-7
Kempe & Thornton 304
Kempe, James 304
Kent, Charles 386
Killen, Jacob A. . .125, 126, 250, 251
Killen, William 250
Killpatrick, Dr. James 318
_____ . The Case of Miss Mary
Roche, who was inoculated
June 28, 1738 318
_____ . A Full and Clear Reply to
Doct. Thomas Dale 322
Kinloch, Francis. Eulogy on George
Washington 335
Kinnier, D. 278
Kinsey, John 145
Kirk, Thomas 202, 215, 217, 218
Kline, Goerge 86-87
Klopstock, _____ . Messiah 239
Kneass, W. 93
Kneeland & Green 115
Koch, _____ 22
Kollock & Arnett 237
Kollock, Shepard 236-37, 239
Krider, _____ 361

Lackington, J. Confessions . . . 217
Lahn, Jacob 80
Lake George Watchman, Caldwell,
New York 220
Lambdin, _____ 94
Lancaster & Mumford 383, 385
Lancaster Correspondent, Lancaster,
Penna 80
Lancaster Journal, Lancaster, Pa.303
Lancaster, William . .383, 385, 386-88
398
Lancaster Wochenblatt, Lancaster,
Penna 80

Lancasterische Zeitung, Lancaster
Pa. (or Lancastersche Zeitung)47, 79
Landsmanns Wochenblatt, Das, Lancaster,
Penna 80
Langworthy, Edward 124
Lansingburgh Gazette, Lansingburgh,
New York 197
Lansingburgh Recorder, Lansingburgh,
New York 196, 206
see also Tiffany's Recorder, Lans.
Lawrence, Daniel 218, 235
Laws, acts of assembly, etc. see under
each state, and under U.S.; see
also under specific title, Laws ...
or Acts . . .
Laws and Acts of the General Assembly
for their Majesties Province of
New York 138
Laws of Maryland, edited by Thomas
Bacon 115-16
Laws of the Government of New-Castle,
Kent and Sussex, Upon Delaware.
Vol. II 246, 248
Laws Of the Province of Pennsylvania
Collected into One Volumn, By
Order of the Governour and Assem-
bly of the said Province 14
Layton, Dr. 98
Leakin, Thomas 274
Leavenworth, David 179
Lee, Charles 66, 123, 124
_____ . Some Queries, Political and
Military, Humbly Offered to the
Consideration of the Public 123
Lee, Chauncey. The American Accomp-
tant 197
Leeds, Daniel. An Almanack for the
Year . . . 1687 4
_____ . _____ 1688 5
_____ . The Second Part of the
Mystery of Fox-Craft 13
Leibert, Peter 76
L'Enfant, Pierre Charles 258, 260
Leonard, Robert, & Co. 213
Lepper & Stettinius 83
Lepper, William Daniel 83
Letter, from the Reverend Mr. George
Whitefield, to the Reverend Mr.

John Wesley, in Answer to his
Sermon Intitled Free Grace, A.194
"Letters from a Farmer," by John
Dickinson.................23, ?148
"Letters from Phocion," by
Alexander Hamilton............163
Lewis & Crowell...................205
Lewis & Horner....................165
Lewis & Ryan......................165
Lewis & Schermerhorn..............211
Lewis Eldad.............199, 205, 211
Lewis, H. C.......................274
Lewis, J. V.......................360
Lewis, Joseph.....................240
Lewis, Matthew G. Alfonso, King
of Castile....................272
Lewis, Richard..............112, 114
_____. Carmen Seculare........112
_____, tr. The Mousetrap, or the
Battle of the Cambrians and
Mice..........................112
Lewis, William.........163, 165, 166
Libel Act of 1791 (England)......149
Lilly, W., tr. The Book of Knowl-
edge Treating of the Wisdom of
the Ancients, by Erra Pater...206
Little, William...................217
Livingston, William (N.J. Gov.)...234
Lloyd, David........................9
Lloyd, Thomas (Lt. Gov of N.J.?)....8
Locke, John.......................374
Lodowick, Charles.................135
Logan, James...................12, 39
_____, tr. Cato's Moral Distichs
Englished in Couplets.........39
London Evening Post...............229
Long Island Courier, Brooklyn,
New York......................215
Long Island Star, Brooklyn, N.Y...202
217-18
Long Island Weekly Intelligencer,
Brooklyn, New York............217
Looker, John M...............207, 213
Loomis, George J..................180
Loomis, George J., & Co........180-81
Lopez, M..........................220
Loring & Hollinshead..............356
Loring, Thomas....................356

Lott, Abraham.....................212
Loudon & Shober...................162
Loudon, John................162, 181
Loudon, Samuel...........152, 162-63
181, 183, 354
Loudon, Samuel Jr.................162
Louisville Gazette and Republican
Trumpet, Louisville, Georgia..398
Lovelace, Francis (N.Y. Gov.)..133-34
Lowell, Samuel....................219
Lucas, Alexander..................363
Lucas & Boylan....................363
Ludlow Post-Man, The (Eng.).......278
Luther, Heinrich Ehrenfried....72, 74
77, 78
Luther typefoundry.............69, 75
Lynchburg Weekly Gazette, Lynchburg,
Virginia......................304
Lynchburg Weekly Museum, Lynchburg,
Virginia......................304
Lyon & Dinmore..............266, 267
Lyon & Field......................302
Lyon, James.......212-13, 265-67, 269
301-2, 304
_____, comp. Masonic Songs,
Oratorio, odes 212-13
Lyon, James, & Co............212, 213
Lyon, Oliver......................210
Lyon, Zebulon.....................210

Madison, James....................275
Magee, James......................348
Mandeville & Westcott.............198
Mandeville, David.................198
Mann & Douglass...................240
Mann, Jacob.......................240
Mansfield & Davis.................333
Mansfield, James..................333
Manual Exercise . . . to be observed
. . . by the Militia of the Pro-
vince of New York, by Guy
Johnson.......................172
Manual of Parliamentary Practice,
by Thomas Jefferson...........271
Markham, J. The Citizen & Country-
man's Experienced Farrier, by

J. Markham and G. Jefferies...248
Markland, J. Typographia. An Ode.....280
Markland, John.........................333
Marsh, Luther...........................220
Martin, Alex.............................128
Martin, Alexander.......................359
Martin, Alexander (N. Car. Gov.)......351
Martin, Francis Xavier.............351-52
_____. Office and Authority of a
    Justice of the Peace, and of Sher-
    iffs, Coroners & c.................352
Marton, William.....163, 165-66, 168, 169
Marvel, Andrew, pseud. see William
    Goddard
Mary, Queen...........................105
    see also William and Mary
Maryland Assembly.....101, 103-10, 114-15
    123-24, 278
_____. Proceedings............109-110
Maryland Chronicle, Frederick, Md.....129
Maryland Gazette, Annapolis, Md..110, 112
    279, 282
Maryland Gazette, Annapolis, Md. (2d)
    115-20, 291
Maryland Gazette, Frederick, Md.......129
Maryland Gazette & Annapolis Advertiser,
    Annapolis, Maryland..........125, 297
Maryland Gazette; or the Baltimore
    General Advertiser, Baltimore, Md.
    125-26, 250, 297
Maryland Governor......105, 107, 110, 115
    Charles Calvert...................110
Maryland Herald, Hagerstown, Md.......131
Maryland Herald and Eastern Shore
    Intelligencer, Easton, Maryland...130
Maryland Journal......................260
Maryland Journal and Baltimore Adver-
    tiser, Baltimore, Md..24, 120, 122-27
    251
Maryland laws, acts of assembly, etc.
    107-10, 114-17, 278, 282, 310
Maryland Muse, The....................114
Maryland Register, Rockville, Md......303
Maryland State printing.......101, 109-10
    141, 278
Mason, William........................327
Masonic Songs . . . , James Lyon, comp.
    212-13
Masons and Anti-Masons.........38-38, 116
Massachusetts Gazette, Boston, Mass...165
Massachusetts Governor Winthrop.......115

Maxwell, _____...................367
Mayer, Benjamin.....................83
Mayer, Salomon...................83, 86
Mayer, Solomon......................77
Mears, _____.....................359
Mecom, Benjamin...........44-46, 152
    229, 231-33
Mecom, Jane Franklin................44
Mehlenberg, _____...............75
Mein & Fleeming.....................163
Mentz, William......................67
Mercer & Carter.....................303
Mercer, Robert......................303
Merchant & Trader's Security......246
Merchants' Daily Advertiser, Phila-
    delphia, Pennsylvania..........56
Mercury, Pittsburgh, Penna.....94, 97
Meredith, _____..............28-29
Meredith & Franklin.....19, 20, 28-29
    32, 310
Meredith, Hugh......19, 20, 24, 28-29
    32, 39, 310
Mershon, John...................235-36
Mesplet, Fleury.....................64
Messenger, Waynesburgh, Penna......98
Messiah, by Klopstock.............239
Mey, Cornelius Jacobsen...........221
Military Collections and Remarks,
    by Major Donkin...............159
Miller, _____...................235
Miller, David C....................213
Miller, Henry (or Müller)46-7, 60, 67
    78-79
Miller, James M....................213
Miller, John.......................333
Miller, John Henry see Henry Miller
Miller, Peter.......................48
Miller Peter (Jabez)...........76, 79
Miller, William A..................252
Mills & Hicks.................163, 165
Mills, Nathaniel.............163, 165
Minerva, Beaver, Pennsylvania......97
Minerva, New York, New York.......239
Minerva, Philadelphia, Penna......128
Minerva, Raleigh, North Carolina..363
Minorca, Island, Gov. William
    Cosby...........................142
Minuet, Peter, (New Amsterdam Gov)132
Minut, Alexander...................242
Mirror, Erie, Pennsylvania.........98
Mirror, Newburg, N.Y..............204

Mirror of the Times, Wilmington,
    Delaware......................252
Miser and Enthusiast, A Novel, The
                                272
Mitchell & Buel................185-86
Mitchell, Isaac...........179, 185-86
                        189, 190, 192
Mite of Praise, The...............253
Modern Chivalry, "Containing the Ad-
    ventures of Captain John Farrago,
    and Teague O'Regan, his Servant"
                                91
Modest Enquiry into the Nature and
    Necessity of a Paper Currency,
    by Benjamin Franklin........28-29
Moffitt & Lyon....................210
Moffitt, Robert....178, 179, 196, 210
Moffitt, Robert, & Co........196, 210
Mohawk Advertiser, Schenectady,
    New York.....................209
Mohawk Mercury, Schenectady, N.Y..208
Moliere...........................374
Monitor, Athens, New York......218-19
Monitor, Washington, D. C.........273
Monitor, Wilmington, Delaware.....251
Montauk Indian catechism..........133
Montgomery, James.................240
Monthly Herald, Augusta, Ga.......398
Montreal Gazette, Montreal, Can....64
Moore, John. Various Views of
    Human Nature...............214-15
Moore, Maurice. Justice and Policy
    of Taxing the American Colonies,
    In Great Britain, Considered..349
Moravian Church (United Brethren)..82
More, Benjamin....................264
Morning Herald, New Bern, N. Car..354
Morris, Anthony.................6, 9
Morris County Gazette, Morristown,
    New Jersey...................240
Morris, Lewis.............142, 143
Morris, Lewis, Jr.................143
Morris-Town Herald, Morristown,
    New Jersey...................240
Morrison, Gawn, pseud. see Hugh
    Henry Brackenridge
Morse, Jedidiah. American
    Geography....................239

Morton & Horner...................163
Morton, John................168, 169
Morton, Thomas. Speed the Plough..271
Morton, William.......63, 163, 165-66
Most Important Question, What is
    Truth, The, by Samuel Jones...278
Mouse-Trap, or the Battle of the
    Cambrians and Mice, The, by
    Richard Lewis................112
Mowbray, Dr.......................318
Mowry, Charles.....................97
M. T. Cicero's Cato Major, or his
    Discourse of Old-Age: With
    Explanatory Notes..............39
Muhlenberg, H. M...................34
Müller, Henry, see Henry Miller
Mullin, Lancelot A...........302, 359
Mumford, _____ 383, 385
Murphy & Bowen....................126
Murphy, Maurice.............126, 360
Murray, Lindley...................212
_____ . English Grammar, Abridge-
    ment......................193, 202
_____ . English Reader.187,197, 214
_____ . _____ . Introduction. 187
_____ . _____ . Sequel.......187
_____ . English Spelling Book...187
Murrey, H...........................2
Muscipula, sive Kambpomyomaxia, by
    Edward Holdsworth............112
Museum & Georgetown Advertiser,
    Georgetown, D. C.........273, 274
Museum and Washington and Georgetown
    Daily Advertiser, D. C...262, 265
                                269
Museum of Delaware, Wilmington,
    Delaware.....................252

McArthur & Courtney...............304
McArthur, John....................304
McCahan, James.....................98
McClean, John S....................87
M'Clellan, Robert..................86
McComb, John........................8
McConnell, Cephas S..............214
McCorkle, Samuel Eusebius. Four

Discourses on the General Prin-
ciples of Deism and Revelation
Contrasted......................361
_____. Three Discourses on the
Terms of Christian Communion....361
McCorkle, William.....................97
McCulloch, John.......................91
McDonald & Buel......................197
McDonald & Moffitt............178, 196
MacDonald, Donald.......63, 163-65, 331
McDonald, John...........177-78, 196-97
McDonald, John, & Co.................178
McDuffee, Daniel..........186, 190, 199
McFarlan, Andrew...............327, 335
MacGee, James.....................21-22
MacGee, Thomas.......................22
McGlashan, Daniel....................180
McIntyre, Patrick...................304-5
McIver, John......................333-34
McIver, John Jr.....................351
McKennie, Clement...................299
McKennie, John H....................299
McKenzie & Westcott.................243
McKenzie, Alexander.............242-43
Maclean & Webster..........174, 293-94
Maclean, Archibald..................294
Maclean, D...........................94
Maclean, John..................174, 293
Maclean, M...........................94
McMillan, Alexander (M'Millan)......395
                                 397-98
McMullin, John.......................305

Narrative of an Attempt made by the
French of Canada upon the Moha-
ques Country....................138
National Gazette, Philadelphia,
Pennsylvania...............169, 242
National Intelligencer and Washington
Advertiser, D. C........266-75, 363
National Magazine, Richmond, Va.....301
National Magazine, or Cabinet of the
United States, Georgetown, D. C.
                             266-67, 301
Navigator, Pittsburgh, Pa............93
Neale & Kammerer....................235

Neale & Lawrence....................235
Neale, Isaac........................235
Necessity of an Early Religion, The,
by Thomas Bray.................107
Nelson, Joseph...............189, 190
Nelson, Richard.....................190
Nelson, Thomas......................189
Nelson, Thomas, & Son..............189
Nelson, William. "Some New Jersey
Printers . . . .".........224-25
Nepos...............................374
Neu-Eingerichteter Americanischer
Geschichts-Calender............47
Neue Philadelphische Correspondenz,
Philadelphia, Penna............67
Neue Unpartheyische Baltimore Bote
und Marylander Staats-Register,
Baltimore, Maryland..........127
Neue Unpartheyische Lancaster Zeit-
ung, Lancaster, Penna..........80
Neue Unpartheyische Readinger Zeit-
ung, Reading, Penna............82
Neuer Hauswirthschafts Calender....83
Neuer Unpartheyischer Eastoner Bothe
Easton, Penna..................83
Nevill, Samuel......................229
New American Magazine, Woodbridge,
New Jersey................150, 229
New Brunswick Gazette, New Brunswick,
New Jersey.....................239
New-England Courant, Boston, Mass.
                               · 25, 29-30
New-England Magazine, Boston, Mass.45
New England Primer......197, 203, 212
                              214, 215
New-England Psalm-Book..............45
New-England's Spirit of Persecution
Transmitted to Pennsilvania, And
the Pretended Quaker found Per-
secuting the True Christian Qua-
ker, in the Tryal of Peter Boss,
George Keith, Thomas Budd, and
William Bradford..............137
New Jersey Assembly.......227, 232-34
_____. Proceedings.....227, 232
New Jersey Federalist, New Brunswick,
New Jersey.....................239
New-Jersey Gazette, Burlington,NJ.234

moved to Trenton, N.J.......234-36
New Jersey Governor
    William Franklin...........22, 231
    William Livingston..............234
New-Jersey Journal, Chatham, NJ.236-37
New-Jersey Journal, Elizabethtown,
    New Jersey......................237
New Jersey laws, acts, etc.
              20, 28, 222-240
New Jersey Lt. Governor
    Thomas Lloyd.....................8
New-Jersey Magazine, Burlington,NJ.235
New Jersey State Gazette, Trenton,
    New Jersey......................235
New Jersey State Gazette, Trenton,
    New Jersey (2d).............235-36
New Jersey state printing....19-20, 28
          37, 138, 148-50, 222, 227
New System of Mercantile Arithmetic,
    by Michael Walsh................93
New System of Philosophy; or the
    Newtonian Hypothesis...........188
New-Windsor Gazette, New Windsor,
    New York.......................212
New York Assembly..7, 134, 135, 143-44
        146, 148, 154, 159, 161, 183
    _____. Committee of Safety......181
    _____. Proceedings.........154, 156
New York Chronicle, NYC...163, 172
New-York Columbian, NYC.............217
New York Constitution..............162
New York Daily Gazette.NYC.........294
New-York Evening Post, NYC.........141
                148, 152
New York Evening Post, NYC (2d)
              63, 165, 217
New-York Gazette, NYC..140-43, 149-50
New-York Gazette, NYC (2d).........152
New-York Gazette, NYC (3d).........152
New-York Gazette & the Weekly Mercury
    New York City.....152, 154, 158-59
    in Newark.......................236
    Royalist, in NYC................236
New-York Gazette; or, the Weekly
    Post-Boy......22, 149-52, 160, 227
New York Gazetteer, and Country
    Journal, New York City....237, 240

New York Gazetteer, or Northern
    Intelligencer, Albany, N.Y.173-74
New York Governor
    Edmund Andros............134, 137
    DeWitt Clinton.................176
    William Cosby..............142-46
    Thomas Dongan.................134
    Benjamin Fletcher.....8-9, 135-38
                  140, 172
    Francis Lovelace...........133-34
    Peter Minuet..................132
    Richard Nicolls...............133
    Peter Stuyvesant..............133
    Rip Van Dam...................142
New-York Journal or General Adver-
    tiser, NYC..150, 160-62, 183, 186
    moved to Kingston, N.Y........183
    moved to Poughkeepsie, N.Y....183
New York laws, acts of assembly, etc.
             138, 149, 156, 186
    _____. Albany...............172-73
    _____. New York........162-63, 215
New York Mercury, NYC........154, 156
New York Mercury, NYC........165, 166
New York Packet, NYC.........152, 164
    moved to Fishkill, N.Y...162, 181
New York Pacquet, NYC.........45, 152
New York Morning Post, NYC.....165-66
New York Morning Post and Daily
    Advertiser, NYC...............166
New York state printing..52, 133, 135
        137-38, 148, 152, 156, 161
        168, 169, 181, 183, 186
New York Weekly Journal, NYC......142
               143-45, 148
New-York Weekly Post Boy, NYC.52, 149
               160, 227
Newark Gazette, Newark, N.J.......236
Newark Republican Herald, Newark
    New Jersey.....................236
Newbern Gazette, Newbern, N. Car..354
Newbern Herald, Newbern, N. Car.354-5
Newburgh Packet,Newburgh, N.Y.....204
Newburgh Republican, Newburgh, N.Y.
                  198, 205
Newcastle Argus, Newcastle, Del...253
Newton, Thomas. Dissertations on

the Prophecies................239
Nicolls & Lowell................219
Nicolls, George W................219
Nicolls, Richard................133
Nicolson, _____. (So. Car. Gov)307
Nicolson & Prentis................295
Nicolson, Thomas............290, 295
297, 299, 300
Niles, Hezekiah..128-9, 248, 250, 251
Niles' Weekly Register, Baltimore,
Maryland......................129
Niles, William Ogden............129
Norfolk & Portsmouth Chronicle,
Norfolk, Virginia............294
Norfolk & Portsmouth Gazette,
Norfolk, Virginia............294
Norfolk & Portsmouth Journal,
Norfolk, Virginia............293
Norfolk Gazette, Norfolk, Va......294
Norfolk Herald, Norfolk, Va.......294
Norman, William E............193, 194
Norris, Isaac.....................13
North, _____ 243
North Carolina Assembly..21, 337, 338
342, 344, 346, 352, 359
_____. Proceedings...338, 356, 358
_____. House of Burgesses.
Journal......................340
North Carolina Centinel, Fayettes-
ville, North Carolina....359, 360
North Carolina Chronicle, Fayettes-
ville, North Carolina....355, 359
North Carolina Circular, New Bern,
North Carolina................354
North Carolina Gazette, Hillsboro,
North Carolina............348, 358
North-Carolina Gazette, New Bern,
North Carolina..........340, 342
346, 348, 351
North Carolina Gazette, New Bern,
North Carolina (2d)...........351
North-Carolina Gazette and Weekly
Post-Boy, Wilmington, North
Carolina..............22, 348, 355
North Carolina Governor......21, 342
Dobbs..........342, 344, 348, 349
Johnston...................337-38
Alexander Martin..............351

North Carolina Intelligencer,
Fayettesville, N. Car........360
North-Carolina Journal, Halifax,
North Carolina.352, 354, 356, 358
North Carolina Journal, Fayettes-
ville, North Carolina........360
moved to Raleigh, N. Car......360
North Carolina laws, acts of assembly
etc.........337-38, 340, 346, 348
352, 356, 358, 359
North Carolina Magazine, New Bern,
North Carolina................342
North Carolina Mercury, Salisbury,
North Carolina................361
North-Carolina Minerva, Fayettes-
ville, North Carolina........354
moved to Raleigh, N. Car.354, 363
North Carolina state printing.....340
Northern Budget, Lansingburgh,
New York............179, 197, 210
moved to Troy, N.Y..197, 210, 211
Northern Centinel, Lansingburgh,
New York............175, 194
moved to Albany, N.Y..........194
Northern Centinel, Salem, N.Y.....207
Northern Herald, Plattsburg, N.Y..219
Northern Politician, Poughkeepsie,
New York............189, 190
Northern Post, Salem, N.Y........207
Northern Whig, Hudson, N.Y.....192-93
Norwich Packet, Norwich, Conn.....163
Nova Scotia Packet: and General
Advertiser, Shelburne, N.S.....61
Nuthead, Dinah............104-05, 277
Nuthead, Susan....................105
Nuthead, William.100, 101, 103-4, 105
107, 277, 278-279
_____, family............100, 104
Nuthead, William, Jr..............105

Observations on the Divine Attri-
butes, by A. M. Toplady........86
Observatory, Richmond, Virginia...229
O'Connor, James..................294
Of Turnip and Pea Fallows, by
by Richard Parkinson..........271

Office and Authority of a Justice
    of the Peace, and of Sheriffs,
    Coroners, &c., The, by Francis
    Xavier Martin..................352
O'Flynn, Captain...................251
Oglethorpe, James Edward.....366, 372
Ohio Navigator, The Pittsburgh, Pa.93
Oley, Dinah Nuthead Devoran.......105
Oley, Sebastian....................105
Olio, Georgetown, D. C.............272
Orange County Gazette, Goshen,
    New York....................198, 205
    moved to Newburgh, N.Y........205
Orange County Gazette, Newburgh,
    New York....................204, 212
Orange County Gazette, and Newburgh
    Public Advertiser, NewBurgh,NY205
Orange County Patriot, Goshen,
    New York....................198-99, 205
Orange County Patriot: or, The
    Spirit of Seventy-Six, Newburgh,
    New York....................198, 205
Orange County Republican, Goshen,
    New York.......................198
Orange County Republican, Wards-
    bridge, New York...............219
Orange Eagle, Goshen, N.Y.........198
Orange Patrol, Goshen, N.Y........198
Oratio Inauguralis, by John Blair
    Smith..........................208
Oration on the Death of General
    George Washington, An.........335
Ormrod & Conrad.....................95
Osborn, John C.....................354
Osborn, Selleck....................200
Oswald & Brown.....................162
Oswald, Eleazer.66, 67, 123, 124, 162
Oswald, Elizabeth Holt..............66
Oswald, John Clyde. Benjamin Frank-
    lin, Printer................47, 52
Otsego Herald, Otsego, N.Y........206
Ovid...............................374

Packard, B. D......................180
Packard, Robert....................180
Paine, G...........................203
Paine, S. & G......................203

Paine, Thomas. The American Crisis..181
_____. Compact Maritime.........271
Palladium of Freedom, Baltimore, Md.126
Palladium of Liberty, Morristown,
    New Jersey.....................240
Palmer, Samuel......................27
Pamela, by Samuel Richardson....39, 149
Paper containing Exceptions against
    some things in the present mode
    of administration & Receiving
    the Lord's Supper in most of our
    Presbyterian Societies..........78
Paper mills and making....7, 22, 72, 76
    77, 174-75, 212, 237, 252, 266
Paraphrastical Exposition on a Letter
    From a Gentleman in Philadelphia
    To his Friend in Boston Concerning
    a certain Person who compared him-
    self to Mordecai...............137
Parker & Bliss.....................211
Parker & Holt......................160
Parker & Weyman............149, 150, 152
Parker, Hyde..................388, 390
Parker, James..22, 24, 44, 45-46, 49-50
    52-53, 119, 121, 149-50, 152
    154, 156, 160, 161, 227, 228
    229, 231, 232, 233, 234
_____, family................231, 233
_____, wife......................231
Parker, Samuel.....................150
Parker, Samuel Franklin...150, 231, 233
Parker, William S..................211
Parkinson, Richard. Of Turnip & Pea
    Fallows........................271
Parks & Hall..................112, 279
Parks & Kinnier....................278
Parks, Benjamin....................272
Parks, Eleanor................278, 284
Parks, William....108, 109-10, 112, 114
    115, 278-84, 286, 290,292
    310, 312, 338, 340
Parks, William the younger.........278
Parris, Alexander..................313
Parsons, Chester...................187
Parthenopolis (fictitious imprint,
    see also Ephrata Brethren).......77
Pascal, Blaise.....................374
Pasteur, John I....................355

Pasteur, John S.....................354
Pastime, Schenectady, N.Y.........209
Pastoral Letter, from the Synod of
    the Carolinas, to the Churches
    under their care...............360
Pastorius, Francis Daniel...........9
Pastorius, Johann Daniel.......68, 75
Pater, Erra. The Book of Knowledge
    Treating of the Wisdom of the
    Ancients, translated by W. Lilly
                                  206
Paterculus, Veiieius...............374
Paterson, William, editor of New
    Jersey laws...................240
Patomak Almanack, or, the Washington
    Ephemeris for . . . 1793......258
Patterson & Lambdin................94
Patterson, Edgar...................274
Patterson, Robert...................94
Patton, William...................126
Paul & Thomas.....................218
Payne, John Howard.................209
Pechin & Niles....................128
Pechin, William...................128
Pelosi, Vincent M...................67
Pelosi's Marine List, Philadelphia,
    Pennsylvania....................67
Penn, William.....1-4, 6, 12, 68, 222
Penniman, Obadiah............178, 211
Penniman, Obadiah & Co...........211
Pennington, Aaron.................236
Pennsylvania Assembly.2-6, 10, 13, 16
                  28-29, 72, 75, 145
Pennsylvania Chronicle, York, Pa...86
Pennsylvania Chronicle and Universal
    Advertiser, Philadelphia, Pa.
            23-24, 45, 61, 120, 236
Pennsylvania Evening Post, Philadel-
    phia, Pennsylvania..........61-62
Pennsylvania Evening Post, and Daily
    Advertiser, Philadelphia, Pa...62
Pennsylvania Gazette, Philadelphia,
    Pa...29-33, 37, 39, 49-50, 57, 60
                        84, 244-46
    moved to York, Pa..............84
Pennsylvania Governor...............6
    Benjamin Fletcher.....8-9, 135-38
                            140, 172

Benjamin Franklin..............54
William Keith...............26-27
Pennsylvania Herald, York, Pa.86, 303
Pennsylvania Journal, Philadelphia,
    Pennsylvania..............56, 60
Pennsylvania law, acts of assembly,
    etc. 6, 10, 13-14, 37, 39
Pennsylvania Ledger, Philadelphia,
    Pennsylvania...........60-61, 62
Pennsylvania Packet, Philadelphia,
    Pennsylvania..59, 60, 62, 80, 125
    moved to Lancaster, Pa.........80
Pennsylvania Staats Courier, Phila-
    delphia, Pennsylvania..........63
Pennsylvania state printing.....6, 29
                            37, 39
Pennsylvanische-Berichte, German-
    town, Pennsylvania.....70, 74, 75
Pennsylvanische Gazette, Die,
    Philadelphia, Pennsylvania.....59
Pennsylvanische Wochenschrift, Die,
    Hanover, Pennsylvania..........83
Pennsylvanische Zeitungs-Blat, Das,
    Lancaster, Pennsylvania........79
Pennsylvanischer Calendar auf das
    1799ste Jahr Christi...........86
Penny Post, Philadelphia, Pa.......45
Pentland & Engles..................94
Pentland, Ephraim..............94, 97
Person, Lewis.....................220
Person, Oliver....................220
Peters, Richard....................33
Petersburg Intelligencer, Petersburg,
    Virginia......................302
"Petition / of Hugh Gaine /," by
    Philip Freneau..........156, 159
Phenix, Staunton, Virginia........304
Philadelphier Teutsche Fama, Phila-
    delphia, Pennsylvania......33, 48
Philadelphier Wochenblatt, Das,
    Philadelphia, Pennsylvania.....82
Philadelphische Zeitung, Philadel-
    phia, Pennsylvania....33, 41, 315
Philadelphische Zeitung; von aller-
    hand Auswartig und einheimischen
    merckwurdigen Sachen, Philadel-
    phia, Pennsylvania......33-34, 48
Philadelphisches Staatsregister,

Philadelphia, ...67, 269
Philanthropist, Westchester,Va.303
Philipse, Adolphus...142, 145, 146
Phillips, Eleazer..............313
Phillips, Eleazer, Jr.....308, 310
                        312, 313, 314
Phinney, Elihu.................206
Pictures of the Passions; or
    Interesting Narratives.....272
Pierie, George W................57
Pinkney, John..........291-92, 344
Pious Guide to Prayer and
    Devotion...................258
Piper, Michael..............108-09
Pittsburg Almanac, or Western
    Ephemeris, For the Year of
    our Lord 1788..............90
Pittsburgh Almanack for the Year
    of our Lord 1802............93
Pittsburgh Gazette, Pittsburgh,
    Pa.......87-88, 90, 91-92, 94
Pittsburgh Magazine Almanack....93
Plain Account of the Ordinance of
    Baptism, A..................214
Plain and Serious Address to the
    Master of a Family on the
    Importance of Family Relig-
    ion, by Phillip Doddridge..200
Plain Dealer, Bridgeton, N.J...234
Pleasants, Samuel..............300
Pleasants, Tarlton W...........302
Plebian, New York, N.Y.........154
Plebian, Kingston, N.Y.185-86, 199
Plough Boy, Albany, N.Y........177
Pocket Almanack for the Year
    1778 by R. Saunders........84
Political Barometer, Poughkeepsie
    New York...........185, 189-90
Political Index, Newburgh, NY..205
Political Intelligencer, New
    Brunswick, N.J.............237
    moved to Elizabethtown, NJ.237
Political Mirror, Staunton, Va.
                        301, 304
Political Observatory, Platts-
    burg, New York.............219
Poor Richard's Almanacs..34-36, 84
Poor Robin's Almanack, or the

Maryland Ephemeris for
    . . . 1790.................256
Pope, Alexander.....................374
_____ . Essay on Man............194
Porter, Robert...............251, 252
Post-Angel, Edenton, N.Car........361
Post-Office Law, The..............269
Postal System.........32, 119-25, 134
                        160, 174
Potowmak Almanack, or, the Washing-
    ton Ephemeris for . . . 1793..258
Potter, Paraclete............187, 190
Potter, Sheldon...................187
Poughkeepsie Journal, Poughkeepsie,
    New York......183, 186-87, 189-90
Poughkeepsie Journal and Constitu-
    tional Republican, Poughkeepsie,
    New York......................187
Powell, F. C......................219
Powell, Thomas...............324, 325
Power & Copp.................183, 185
Power & Southwick.................187
Power, Nicholas......183, 185-87, 189
Power, Nicholas & Co...........186-87
Power of the Gospel, in the Conver-
    sion of Sinners, by George
    Keith.........................107
Powers & Seymour..................395
Powers, Titus.....................395
Prange, James.....................235
Pratt & Doubleday.................180
Pratt, Luther.197, 199, 210, 212, 219
Pratt, Luther, & Co..........197, 210
Pratt, Moses......................180
Pray & Bowen......................218
Prentice, Russell............213, 214
Prentis & Baxter..................294
Prentis & Hunter..................302
Prentis & Pleasants...............302
Prentis, William........294, 295, 302
Prentiss, Charles..128, 262, 265, 300
Present for an Apprentice, A......178
Press Restriction Act of 1693(Eng)276
Preston, _____ 252
Pretty Story written in . . . 2774,
    /sic / by Francis Hopkins.....291
Prevost, Augustin.................390
Price & Gird...................300-01

Price, Ellis...................300-01
Priestley, _____.............258
Princeton Packet, Princeton, N.J..242
Promised Seed, The, by William
    Cooper.......................214
Proposals for the Printing of a
    large Bible by William Bradford
                                5-6
Proudfit, Alexander...........207-8
Providence Gazette,
    Providence, Rhode Island.......22
Prowess of the Whig Club, by
    William Goddard..............123
Purdie, Alexander..288, 290, 298, 342
Purdie & Dixon..............288, 290
Pusey, Caleb.............10, 12, 13
_____. Bomb Search'd and found
    stuff'd with False Ingredients.12
_____. Satan's Harbinger
    Encountered...................10
_____. Some brief Observations
    Made on Daniel Leeds his Book..13

Quakers, see Society of Friends
Quequelle & Prange...............235
Quequelle & Wilson...............235
Quequelle, Frederick C...........235

Rabelais (Pract Phillipot).......177
Raleigh Register, Raleigh, N. Car.363
Raleigh, Sir Walter..............276
Ralph, James......................27
Ramsay, David. History of the Rev-
    olution of South Carolina.....235
Ramsey, _____ 355
Randolph & Bunce.................398
Randolph, George F...............398
Rapine, Conrad & Co...........270-72
Rapine, Daniel..........270-71, 275
Raswell, Robert..................334
Ray & Black......................360
Raylton, Tacy (Sowle).............17
Read, _____ 26, 49
Read, Deborah.....................26

Reading Mercury, or Weekly Enter-
    tainer, England..............278
Reading, Thomas..................107
Readinger Adler, Reading, Penna....82
Readinger Zeitung, Reading, Pa....130
Reben, Albert Conrad..............77
Recorder, Lansingburgh, N.Y..196, 210
    moved to Troy, N.Y.......196, 210
Recorder of the Times, Newburgh,
    New York.....................205
Regulations for the Order and Dis-
    cipline of the Troops of the
    United States. Part I.........360
Reiche, Charles C.................67
Remarkable Dream . . . A, by Aaron
    Warner.......................200
Report of the Committee Appointed
    to examine into the Proceedings
    of the People of Georgia, with
    respect to the Province of
    South Carolina...............318
Reporter, Washington, Penna....97, 98
Republican, Petersburg, Va...301, 302
Republican, Plattsburg, N.Y.......219
Republican Citizen, Fredericksburg
    Virginia.................302, 359
Republican Crisis, Albany, New York
                        179, 189, 192
Republican Fountain, Hudson, N.Y..192
Republican Herald, Poughkeepsie,
    New York.................190, 199
Republican Journal, Danbury, Conn.189
Republican Journal, Dumfries, Va..304
Republican Journal, Poughkeepsie,
    New York.................186, 189
Republican Luminary, Wythe Court
    House, Virginia..............305
Republican Press, Leesburg, Va....305
Republican Star, Easton, Md.......130
Republican Telescope, Ballston Spa,
    New York.....................213
Republican Watch-Tower, N.Y., N.Y.204
Reveille, Elizabethtown, N.Y......220
Revolutionary War..152, 156, 163, 164
                    166, 173, 234, 236
                    259, 292, 331, 333
Reyners, Joseph.................10-13

Reynolds, George...............86-87
Reynolds, John (Ga. Gov.)........366
Reynolds, John P................207
Reynolds, Linus J...........219, 220
Reynolds, Samuel................199
Rhoads, Asa. An American Spelling
    Book.........................218
Richard Saunders see Poor Richard
Richards, George, & Co...........300
Richards, Philip...................2
Richardson, Andrew...............92
Richardson, Samuel. Pamela....39, 149
Richmond and Manchester Advertiser,
    Richmond, Virginia...........300
Richmond Chronicle, Richmond, Va..299
Riggs & Stevens..................209
Riggs, Isaac................209, 213
Riggs, Stephen S................209
Rights of Man, Frederick, Md......130
Rights of Man, Newburgh, N.Y......190
                              204-5
Riley, Isaac.....................219
Riley, William...................252
Rind & Prentiss.............262, 265
Rind, Clementina.................291
Rind, William.........116, 233, 290-1
Rind, William Alexander.262, 265, 269
                    272, 273, 274
Rind, William Alexander Jr...273, 274
Rising Sun, Kingston, New York....185
Risley & Skinner.................252
Risley, Jeremiah B...............252
Rittenhouse, _____.............88
Rittenhouse, Nicholas.............7
Rittenhouse, William..............7
Rivington, James........159, 163, 164
Rivington's New-York Gazette, New
    York, N.Y....................164
Rivington's New-York Gazetteer; or
    the Connecticut, New-Jersey,
    Hudson's-River, and Quebec
    Weekly Advertiser, NY, NY.....164
Robert, Michael..................270
Roberts, Daniel. Some Memoirs of
    the Life of John Roberts.....218
Roberts, Sylvester...............192
Roberts, Sylvester, & Co.........192
Roberts, T.......................86

Robertson, Alexander..63-64, 163-65
                        172-73, 220
Robertson, James......63-64, 163-65
                  172-73, 220, 331, 333
Robertson, Macdonald & Cameron..331
Robertsons & Trumbull...........163
Robinson & Little...............217
Robinson Crusoe by Daniel Defoe.156
Robinson, William C.............217
Rockbridge Repository, Lexington,
    Virginia....................305
Rollins, _____ 374
Rook, T.........................248
Rootes, Philip..................302
Rose, Aquila.................17, 25
Ross, William...................269
Roulstone, George............358-60
Royal American Gazette, NYC......63
                            163-65
Royal Bahama Gazette, Nassau....329
Royal Gazette, Charleston, S.C..329
Royal Gazette, Jamaica..........329
Royal Gazette, N.Y., N.Y...164, 165
Royal Gazette and New-Brunswick
    Advertiser, St. John, N.B.
                          63, 164
Royal Georgia Gazette, Savannah,
    Georgia..........388, 390, 391
Royal Pennsylvania Gazette,
    Philadelphia, Penna.....63, 163
Royal St. John's Gazette, St. John,
    New Brunswick...............165
Royal South-Carolina Gazette,
    Charleston, SC.......63, 164-65
                          331, 333
Royle, Joseph, & Co.............288
Rudd & Stockholm................190
Rudd, Reuben B..................190
Ruddiman, Thomas. The Rudiments
    of the Latin Tongue.........346
Rudiments of the Latin Tongue,
    The, by Thomas Ruddiman......346
Rules and Articles for the Better
    Government of the Troops . . .
    of the United States of
    America......................269
Rumsey, David Jr................207
Rural Casket, Poughkeepsie, NY..187

Rural Visitor & Saratoga Adver-
    tiser, Ballston Spa, N.Y....213-14
Russell, Caleb.....................240
Russell, Charles...................240
Russell, Henry P...................240
Rusticoat, Robert, pseud., see
    Harry Croswell
Rutgers University.................239
Ryan, John.........................165

Saalhof Pietists....................68
Sag Harbor. Literary Society. Con-
    stitution......................202
St. John, James.............308, 310
Saints' Everlasting Rest, The, by
    Richard Baxter.................217
Salem Gazette, Salem, Mass........331
Salley, A. S., Jr. "The First
    Presses of South Carolina."....308
Sallust............................374
Sample, William.....................97
Sampson, Chittenden & Croswell
                        191, 193, 194
Sampson, Ezra......................191
_____ . The Beauties of the Bible193
_____ . Brief Remarker on the Ways
    of Man.........................193
_____ .   . (another ed.)..194
_____ . Youth's Companion (2 eds)193
Saratoga Advertiser, Ballston Spa,
    New York.....................213-14
Saratoga Courier, Ballston Spa, NY.214
Saratoga Gazette, Saratoga Springs,
    New York.....................219-20
Saratoga Journal, Ballston Spa, NY.214
Saratoga Patriot, Ballston Spa, NY.214
Saratoga Register: or, Farmer's
    Journal, Ballston Spa, NY......213
Saratoga Republican, Ballston
    Spa, New York..................214
Saratoga Sentinel, Saratoga
    Springs, New York..............220
Satan's Harbinger Encountered, by
    Caleb Pusey.....................10
Sauer, Christopher, see Christopher
    Saur
Saunders, Richard, pseud, see Ben-
    jamin Franklin, Poor Richard

Saunders, Robert Jr...............131
Saur, see also under Sower
Saur, Christopher I.....22, 62, 68-78
                                  127
_____ , wife (Sister Marcella)...69
Saur, Christopher II....69, 74-75, 76
Saur, Christopher III..............75
Saur Foundry.......................75
Saur, Peter........................75
Savoy, Duke of.....................37
Scharf, J. Thomas. History of Mary-
    land...........................131
Schenectady Gazette, Schenectady,
    New York.......................209
Schermerhorn, Ryer...........209, 211
Schlichting, Christian..............86
Schnee, Jacob.......................94
Schneider & Gerrisch................82
Schneider, Jacob.................82-83
Schultz & Barber...................204
Schultz & Lott.....................212
Schultz, Jacob...............204, 212
Schütz, Christian...................69
Schuyler, Peter....................135
Scioto Gazette, Chillicothe, Ohio.303
Scourge of Aristocracy, Staunton,
    Virginia...................301, 304
Scull & Boyd........................90
Scull & Hall........................88
Scull, John......................88-93
Scull, John I....................91, 94
Seabury, Samuel A................202-3
Searmoin chuaidh a liobhairt aig
    an Raft-Swamp, by Dugald
    Crawford.......................360
Seaton, William Winston......268, 363
Second Letter to . . . George White-
    field concerning the Accompts
    of the Orphan-House in Georgia323
Second Part of the Mystery of
    Fox-Craft, by Daniel Leeds.....13
Seidensticker, Oswald. The First
    Century of German Printing in
    America, 1728-1830.............48
Select and Fugitive Poetry, comp.
    by Richard Dinmore.......267, 272
Sellers, William...50, 57, 60, 84, 86
Sellers, William Jr.................57
Seneca.............................374
Series of Letters . . . to the Rev.

Adam Freeman, A, by Rev.
  Stephen B. Balch..............271
Serle, Ambrose.................158-59
Setauket. Franklinian Library.
  Catalog......................202
Sewel, William..............17-19, 28
_____ . The History of the . . .
  Quakers..................17-19, 28
Seymour & Woolhopter.........395, 397
Seymour, Gurden I..................395
Shaftsbury Baptist Assn. Minutes..212
Shakespeare, William..............374
Sheffield Register, England.......363
Shelton, John.....................284
Sheppard, Thomas.............327, 334
Sherman & Mershon.................235
Sherman, George.................235-36
Sherman, Mershon & Thomas.........235
Shippen, Edward.....................9
Shober, Frederick....118-20, 152, 162
Sibley & Howard..............359, 360
Sibley & Mullin...................359
Sibley, Howard & Roulstone........360
Sibley, John..............302, 359-60
Sibley, John, & Co...........359, 360
Six Nations.......................170
Skinner, Daniel...................175
Skinner, Elisha W.................175
Skinner, Hezekiah.................175
Skinner, Robert...................252
Sleight, Henry C.............217, 218
Slump, John Martin.336, 361, 363, 365
Smith & Cossens...................322
Smith & Jackson...................128
Smith & Price.....................300
Smith, John.......................128
Smith, John.......................300
Smith, Capt. John..................99
Smith, John Blair. Oratio Inaugur-
  alis.........................208
Smith, John Erdman......394, 395, 397
Smith, Josiah. The Character and
  Duty of Minister and People...318
Smith, Samuel. The History of the
  Colony of Nova-Caesaria or
  New Jersey..........229, 231, 232
Smith, Samuel Harrison.........267-72
Smith, Thomas..................44, 52

Smith, Thomas Perrin..............130
Smith, William..........143, 145, 338
Smith, Rev. William.............33-34
Smith's History of New Jersey......45
Smylie, James.....................335
Smyth, Albert H., ed. The Writings
  of Benjamin Franklin..........47
Smyth & Edwards...................251
Smyth, William Catherwood....250, 251
Snowden, John M................94, 97
Snowden, Samuel..............268, 301
Society for Propagating Christian
  Knowledge Among the Germans in
  Pennsylvania...............33, 48
Society of Friends.1-9, 12-14, 17, 19
    24, 75, 135, 136, 138, 221-22
_____ . Report of the Yearly
  Meeting. 1686..................4
_____ . _____ . 1710...........13
Some brief Observations Made on
  Daniel Leeds his Book, Entitul-
  ed The Second Part of the Mys-
  tery of Fox-Craft, by Caleb
  Pusey.......................13
Some Memoirs of the Life of John
  Roberts, by Daniel Roberts....218
Some Queries, Political & Military,
  Humbly offered to the Consid-
  eration of the Public, by
  Charles Lee..................123
Sot-Weed Factor; or, a Voyage to
  Maryland, by Ebenezer Cooke...114
Sotweed Redivivus, The, by Ebenezer
  Cooke.......................114
South-Carolina and American General
  Gazette, Charleston, South
  Carolina.................327, 329
South Carolina Assembly.307, 308, 310
    312-14, 316, 325
_____ . Proceedings.............325
South Carolina Gazette, Charleston,
  South Carolina..41, 316, 318, 320
    322, 324, 325, 326
South Carolina Gazette, Charleston,
  South Carolina............312-15
South Carolina Gazette, Columbia,
  South Carolina...............335
South Carolina Gazette; and Country

42

Journal, Charleston, South
    Carolina......................331
South Carolina Gazette and General
    Advertiser, Charleston, S.Car.333
South Carolina Governor
    James Glen....................322
    Robert Johnson........308, 312-14
    _____ Nicholson............307
South Carolina Independent Gazette;
    and Georgetown Chronicle,
    Georgetown, South Carolina....335
South Carolina laws, acts of assembly
    etc........312-13, 315-16, 318-19
South-Carolina State-Gazette,
    Charleston, South Carolina....327
South Carolina Weekly Advertiser,
    Charleston, South Carolina...333
South Carolina Weekly Gazette,
    Charleston, S. Car......327, 333
South Carolina Weekly Journal,
    Charleston, S. Car......312, 313
Southern Centinel and Universal
    Gazette, Augusta, Ga.....395, 397
Southwick, Henry C...176, 178, 186-87
Southwick, Solomon.................176
Southwick, Solomon, Jr.176-79, 186-87
Sower & Gwynn..................76, 127
Sower, Brook W....................305
Sower, Christopher III.62-64, 75, 163
                              165-66
Sower, Daniel......................76
Sower, David.......................76
Sower, Peter................62-64, 75
Sower, Samuel......63, 76, 82, 127-28
Sowle, Andrew....................1, 14
Sowle, Elizabeth....................1
Spafford, Horatio Gates. General
    Geography & Rudiments of Useful
    Knowledge.....................193
Sparrow, Thomas...................116
Spear, John.....................93-94
Speed the Plough, by Thomas
    Morton.......................271
Spelling book, by Dillworth........95
    _____, by Dyche............346
Spencer & Webb...................180
Spencer, Thomas.............196, 197
Spirit of Seventy-Six, Richmond,

Virginia......................274
    moved to Washington, D.C......274
    moved to Georgetown, D.C.274, 275
Spooner, Alden.......200, 202, 217-18
Spooner & Worthington.........217-18
Spooner, Judah Padock.............200
Springer, Zadoc....................97
Squire, Captain...................293
Stamp Act of 1765.....156, 229, 231
                      232, 331, 375
Stanard, Edward C.................274
Stanford, John. Urim & Thummim....215
Star: and Charleston Daily Adverti-
    ser, Charleston, S. Car..334, 355
Starr, Caleb......................251
State Gazette, Trenton, N.J.......235
State Gazette of North Carolina,
    New Bern, North Carolina.352, 359
    moved to Edenton, N.Car..352, 354
                      356, 360, 361
State Gazette of South-Carolina,
    Charleston, S. Car.........326-27
State Gazette of South Carolina,
    Columbia, South Carolina.....335
Statesman, Pittsburgh, Pa..........94
Staunton Spy, Staunton, Va.......304
Stebbins, Francis.................192
Steel & McClean....................87
Steel, James.......................87
Steiner, Melchior............67, 269
Stereotyping.......................46
Sterne, Laurence. Tristram Shandy..91
Stettinius, E......................83
Steuart, Andrew...21-22, 67, 328, 344
                      348-49, 355
Stevens, Isaac....................209
Stevenson, Dr. Henry.............118
Stevenson, James Jr..............207
Stevenson, John L................209
Stewart, Jacob.....................97
Stewart, James H...................59
Stewart, John....................265
Stiemer, Anton.....................80
Stiles, Thomas T...................57
Stockholm & Brownejohn...........190
Stockholm, Derick B..............190
Stockton, _____.................94
Stockwell, _____..............218

Stockwell, Henry...................211
Stoddard & Webster................175
Stoddard, Ashbel.175, 190-1, 193, 194
Stoddard's Diary, or Columbia
    Almanack........................191
Stone & Corss..................192-93
Stone, William L...............192-93
Story & Humphrey's Pennsylvania
    Mercury, Philadelphia, Penna...66
Story, Enoch........................66
Story, Enoch, the younger........119
Strahan, William............44-45, 49
Street, Joseph M., & Co...........273
Strictures on a Pamphlet entitled
    the Case of George M'Intosh,
    Esq.............................383
Strictures on the Second Part of
    the Age of Reason, by Bryan
    Fairfax........................262
Stuyvesant, Peter (New Amsterdam
    Governor).......................133
Suffolk County Herald, Sag Harbor,
    Long Island, N.Y...............200
Suffolk County Recorder, Sag Harbor,
    Long Island, N.Y...............202
Suffolk Gazette, Sag Harbor, Long
    Island, N.Y...............200, 202
Sunday Monitor, Baltimore, Md.....127
Supplement to the Boston Independent
    Chronicle, Passy, France.......53
Sure Guide to Hell................149
Swaine & Miller...................213
Swaine, John.........168-69, 213, 242
Swann, Samuel.....................340
Swift, Jonathan...................374
Sylvanus Americanus, pseud, see
    Judge Samuel Nevill

Tappen, John......................186
Taufscheine (Baptism Certificates).83
Taylard, William..................104
Taylor, Frances. An Epistle to
    Friends to be read in their
    Monthly Meeting.................4
Taylor, Jacob................4, 12-14
    . Almanacs, 1702-1746..12, 13

Taylor, Mahlon....................212
Taylor, Randal....................101
Telegraphe, Carlisle, Penna........87
Telegraphe: and Charleston Daily
    Advertiser, Charleston, S.Car.334
Telegraphe & Daily Advertiser,
    Baltimore, Maryland...........128
Tennery & Stockwell...............218
Tennery, Joseph................218-19
Thomas, ...218
Thomas & Leakin...................274
Thomas & Westcott.................301
Thomas, John......................274
Thomas, John V....................301
Thomas, Isaiah.......178, 290, 327-28
                         349, 350-51
_____, History of Printing...5, 45
    56, 59, 62, 75, 119, 124, 163
    219-20, 233, 246, 248, 288
                         290, 305
Thomas, Isaiah.................235-36
Thompson, John P..............87, 274
Thompson, Thomas...................97
Thornton, Thomas..................304
Thoughts on the Increasing Wealth
    and National Economy of the
    United States of America, by
    Samuel Blodget................271
Three Discourses on the Terms of
    Christian Communion, by Samuel
    Eusebius McCorkle.............361
Throckmorton, William.............304
Tiffany & Wands...................196
Tiffany, Sylvester......196, 197, 206
Tiffany's Recorder, Lansingburgh,
    New York..................196, 206
    Moved to Troy, New York.......210
Time Piece, New York, N.Y.........242
Times, Carlisle, Penna.............87
Times and Political and Commercial
    Evening Gazette, Charleston,
    South Carolina................334
Times, and the Patowmack Packet,
    Georgetown, D.C..255-56, 258, 304
Times of Alexandria, Alexandria, Va.
                                 270
Times, or National Courier, Salem,
    New York...................206-7

Timothee, Louis, see
    Timothy, Lewis, et al.
Timothy & Boden....................326
Timothy & Hughes...................324
Timothy & Mason....................327
Timothy & McFarlan.................327
Timothy & Powell...................324
Timothy & Sheppard.................327
Timothy & Walsh....................326
Timothy, Ann Donavan...............326
Timothy, Benjamin Franklin...322, 325
                              327, 335
Timothy, Charles...................326
Timothy, Elizabeth......41-42, 315-16
                              320, 326
Timothy, Lewis.33, 41-42, 308, 315-20
        , family.............42, 320
Timothy, Peter...42, 318, 320, 322-26
                              331, 366
Timothy, Powell & Hughes..........324
Tod, James........................242
Tom Tell-Truth, pseud., see
    William Goddard
Toplady, A. M. Observations on the
    Divine Attributes..............86
Towne, Benjamin.............23, 61-62
Tracy & Bliss.....................197
Tracy, Gardiner...................197
Travels of True Godliness and Ungod-
    liness, The, by Benjamin
    Keach.........................208
Tree of Liberty, Pittsburgh, Penna.
                          92, 94, 97
Trenton Mercury, Trenton, N.J.....235
Treutlen, John Adam (Ga. Gov.)....381
Trinity Church, New York..137-38, 140
Trisler & Haff....................303
Trisler, George...................303
Tristram Shandy, by Laurence Sterne
                             91
Trott, Nicholas.............316, 319
Troy Gazette, Troy, N.Y......193, 205
                         209, 211
Troy Post, Troy, N.Y..............211
True American, Leesburg, Va.......304
True American, Philadelphia, Pa....57
True Republican, New Bern, N.Car..355
True Republican, Wilmington, N.C.
                         355, 356

Trumbull, John..............163, 172
Truth Advanced in the Correction of
    many Gross & hurtful Errors,
    by George Keith...............138
Truth Rescued from Forgery &
    Falshood . . . , by Samuel
    Jenings........................10
Tucker, William...................179
Two Sermons, on the Certain and
    Final Perseverance of the
    Saints, by Rev. Stephen
    Bloomer Balch.................258
Type and typefounding..63, 69, 72, 75
        76, 77-78, 82, 127-28, 322
    Bache typefoundry..............53
    Sower typefoundry..............63
Type, Hebrew......................137
Typographia, by J. Markland.......280

Ulster County Gazette, Kingston,
    New York......................185
Ulster Gazette, Kingston, N.Y.....185
Union College, Schenectady, N.Y.208-9
Union Gazette, Lynchburg, Va......304
U. S. Congress......64, 254, 255, 264
                         268, 270
        . House. Journal..........269
        . Senate. Journal........269
U. S. Constitution.............175-76
    in Dutch......................175
U. S. Laws...........91-92, 169, 269
U. S. Library of Congress....185, 272
        . Catalog.................272
U. S. printing...............169, 183
United States Spelling Book........93
Universal Gazette, Philadelphia,
    Pennsylvania..................268
    moved to Washington, D.C.268, 274
Universal Instructor in all Arts
    and Sciences: and Pennsylvania
    Gazette, Philadelphia, Pa.
                       20-21, 30
Unpartheyische Reading Adler, Der,
    Reading, Penna.................82
Unpartheyische York Gazette, York,
    Pennsylvania...............83, 86

Urim and Thummim, by John
    Stanford.....................215
Urständlicheund Erfahrungs-Volle
    Hohe Zeugnüsse, by Conrad
    Beissel......................77
Ustick, John G....................305
Ustick, Stephen C.................243

Vallette, Elie. Deputy Commissary's
    Guide........................116
Van Benthuysen, Obadiah...........180
Van Dam, Rip (N.Y. Gov.)..........142
Vandeput, Captain.................156
Vanderburgh, Richard.........186, 189
Van Horne, Philip.................204
Van Veghten, Cornelius............209
Van Veghten, Derick...............209
Various Views of Human Nature, by
    John Moore..................214-15
Vaughan & Coleman.................251
Vaughan, John.....................251
Velnet, Mrs. An Affecting History
    of the Captivity & Suffering
    of 202
Verbesserte Hóch-Deutsche American-
    ische Land und Staats Calendar,
    Der (1785)...................129
Verses Occasioned by the Loss of
    the Brig Sally 199-200
Virgil............................374
Virginia Argus, Richmond, Va......300
Virginia Assembly..114, 277, 279, 282
    286, 288, 295, 297-98, 310, 312
Virginia Centinel, Winchester, Va.303
Virginia Chronicle, Norfolk, Va.
                              260, 294
Virginia Federalist, Richmond,
    Virginia.................262, 265
Virginia Gazette, Alexandria, Va..300
Virginia Gazette, Dumfries, Va....304
Virginia Gazette, on the HMS
    Dunmore......................293
Virginia Gazette, Norfolk, Va.....161
Virginia Gazette, Petersburg, Va..302
Virginia Gazette, Richmond, Va....295
Virginia Gazette, Staunton, Va....304

Virginia Gazette, Williamsburg,
    Virginia...........284, 288, 290
Virginia Gazette, Williamsburg,
    Virginia (2d)..288, 290, 342, 344
Virginia Gazette, Williamsburg,
    Virginia (3d)...........290, 295
    moved to Richmond, Va....290, 295
Virginia Gazette, Williamsburg,
    Virginia (4th)...............291
Virginia Gazette, Winchester, Va..303
Virginia Gazette and Agricultural
    Depository, Dumfries, Va......256
Virginia Gazette and Alexandria
    Advertiser, Alexandria, Va....258
Virginia Gazette & General Adver-
    tiser, Richmond, Va.......299-300
Virginia Gazette and Independent
    Chronicle, Richmond, Va......299
Virginia Gazette, and Public
    Advertiser, Richmond, Va.....299
Virginia Gazette and Richmond and
    Manchester Advertiser, Richmond
    Virginia.....................300
Virginia Gazette & Richmond
    Chronicle, Richmond, Va......299
Virginia Gazette: and Richmond
    Daily Advertiser, Richmond, Va355
Virginia Gazette & Weekly Advertiser,
    Richmond, Va.................295
Virginia Gazette, or Norfolk Intel-
    ligencer, Norfolk, Va........292
Virginia Gazette, or, the American
    Advertiser, Richmond, Va.....299
Virginia Governor.................286
    Sir William Berkeley.....100, 276
    Lord Thomas Culpeper.......276-77
    William Gooch................282
    Lord Francis Howard of Effingham
                          100, 277, 278
    Thomas Jefferson.........297, 298
Virginia Herald, Fredericksburg,
    Virginia.....................302
Virginia Independent Chronicle,
    Richmond, Virginia...........299
Virginia Journal, Alexandria, Va..300
Virginia laws, acts of assembly, etc.
    37, 277, 280, 282, 284, 288, 290
        295, 299, 300, 302, 310

Virginia Miscellany, Williamsburg,
    Virginia......................279
Virginia Miscellany, consisting of
    New Poems, Essays, and Trans-
    lations, on various Subjects..282
Virginia Patriot, Richmond,Va.299-300
Virginia Star, Petersburg, Va.....302
Virginia state printing.......37, 161
                            295, 300
Virginische Volksberichier, und
    Newmarketen Wochenschrift,
    Newmarket, Virginia..........305
Voltaire..........................374
_____. Philosophical Dictionary
                              203-4

Wadsworth & Looker................213
Wadsworth, Horace H...............213
Wagner, Jacob.................274-75
Waldo, Elisha H...................398
Waldo, Francis W..................360
Walker, James.....................303
Walloons.....................132, 170
Walsh, E..........................326
Walsh, Michael. New System of Mer-
    cantile Arithmetic............93
Walton, George....................378
Wands & Honeywood.................196
Wands, William W........196, 197, 207
Warner, Aaron. A Remarkable Dream
    or Vision Experienced on the
    Night of the 20th May, 1799...200
Warner & Hanna....................128
Warner, Isaiah.....................16
Warner, William...................128
Warren Republican, Glen's Falls,
    New York......................220
Washington Advertiser, Washington,
    D. C...........260, 262, 264, 268
Washington City Gazette, Washing-
    ton, D. C.....................275
Washington County Post, Salem, NY.207
Washington Expositor and Weekly
    Intelligencer, Washington,
    D. C....................273, 274
Washington Federalist, Georgetown,
    D. C........262, 265, 269, 272-74

Washington Gazette, Washington,
    D. C..........................264
Washington, George..90, 123, 185, 253
                254, 255, 258, 286, 358
_____. An Address to the People
    of the United States.......252-53
_____. Journal.................286
Washington Museum, Georgetown, DC.262
Washington Patrol, Salem NY.......196
                                206-7
Washington Printing & Bookselling
    Co....................266-67, 272
Washington Register, Salem, NY....207
Washington Spy, Elizabethtown, Md.
                                130-31
Washingtonian, Leesburg, Va.......304
Washingtonian, Washington, Penna...97
Wasp, Hudson, N.Y.................192
Watch Tower, New York, N.Y........154
Waterford Gazette, Waterford, NY..213
Watson & Hall.................354, 356
Watson & Ramsey...................355
Watson, Thomas................354-56
Watterson, George.................275
Watts, John........................27
Waudin, John..................392-94
Way & Groff.........268-69, 271, 272
Way, Andrew.......................269
Way, George.......................269
Way to Wealth, The, by Benjamin
    Franklin......................194
Wayne, Anthony....................391
Webb, George..............20, 37, 308
                            310, 312, 316
Webb, Thomas S....................180
Webbe, John................16, 36-38
Webster & Stoddard..............190-1
Webster, Charles R.173-77, 180, 190-1
                193, 197, 212, 213, 294
Webster, Charles R., & George..174-75
Webster, Charles R., & George, & Co.
                                174
Webster, George...........173-76, 212
Webster, Mary (Pratt).............173
Webster, Matthew..................173
Webster, Noah.....................162
_____. American Spelling Book..212
Webster, Truman...................213
Websters & Skinner (s)............175

Weekly Advertiser, Reading, Pa.....82
Weekly Monitor & American
    Advertiser, Litchfield, Conn..183
Weekly Museum, Baltimore, Md......128
Weekly Price Current, Philadelphia,
    Penna.........................61
Weeks, Stephen B. Press of North
    Carolina.....................340
Weems, Rev. Mason L. (Parson)
    History of the Life . . . of
    General George Washington
                    239, 262, 264
Weiser, _____ 75
Weiser, Conrad....................33
Weiss, Jacob......................69
Weiss, Ludwig.....................48
Welch, Edward..........386, 387, 398
Wells, _____ 218
Wells & Bruce....................327
Wells, John.................327, 329
Wells, Louisa Susannah...........329
Wells, Robert...327-28, 329, 331, 350
Wells, Robert, & Son....327, 330, 333
Wells, William Charles...........329
Wessells, Warnaer................140
_____ , son...................140
West, Stephen. Animadversions on a
    Late Publication, Entitled the
    Duty and Obligation of Christ-
    ians to Marry Only in the Lord
                                181
Westchester Herald, Mt. Pleasant,
    New York.....................215
Westchester Patriot, Mt. Pleasant,
    New York.....................220
Westcott, David M................198
Westcott, James D...........243, 301
Westcott, John...................301
Western Advertiser, Chambersburg,
    Penna........................294
Western Budget, Schenectady, NY...209
Western Carolinian, Salisbury,
    North Carolina...............361
Western Constellation, Catskill,
    New York.....................203
Western Corrector, Washington, Pa..97
Western Press, Mercer, Pa.........98
Western Register, Washington, Pa...97

moved to Uniontown, Pa.........97
Western Spectator, Schenectady, NY209
Western Star, Stockbridge, Mass...178
Western Telegraphe, Washington, Pa.95
Western World, Frankfort, Ky.....273
Westliche Correspondenz, Die,
    Hagarstown, Md...............131
Weygrand, Cornelius...............83
Weygrand, Jacob...................83
Weyman & Gaine...................154
Weyman, William....140, 149, 150, 152
                            154, 156
Wharton, Thomas.............23-24, 61
Whitaker, Robert.................324
White, Father Andrew.............131
White, Thomas W..................273
Whitefield, George................72
_____ . A Letter . . . to the
    Reverend Mr. John Wesley in
    Answer to his Sermon Intitled
    Free Grace...................194
Whitestown Gazette, Whitestown,
    New York.....................186
Whiting, _____ 189
Whiting & Leavenworth..........178-79
Whiting, Backus & Whiting........179
Whiting, Daniel................178-79
Whiting, Daniel & Samuel (firm)...179
Whiting, Leavenworth & Whiting....179
Whiting, Samuel..................179
Whitmarsh, Thomas........41, 308, 310
                        312-15, 327
Wilbur, Solomon Jr..........193, 211
Wiley, David.....................274
Willcocks, Henry.............86, 303
Willets, Jacob...................187
Willett & Davis..................294
Willett, Charles.................294
William and Mary....100-101, 135, 138
William, King....................105
Williams, Eleazer. Gaiatonsera ion-
    teweienstakwa . . . . /Iroquois
    spelling book /..............219
Williams, John...................236
Willis, Nathaniel................303
Willis's Virginia Gazette, Winches-
    ter, Virginia................303
Wills, Henry....352, 354, 356, 358-61

Wills, James................352, 361
Wilmington Centinel, Wilmington,
    North Carolina................355
Wilmington Chronicle, Wilmington,
    North Carolina..........355, 356
Wilmington Courant, Wilmington,
    Delaware.................246, 250
Wilmington Gazette, Wilmington,
    North Carolina................356
Wilson & Baxter...................260
Wilson, George M..................235
Wilson, James..................251-52
Wilson, John......................217
Wilson, Thomas.....190, 205, 260, 294
Winchester Triumph of Liberty,
    Winchester, Virginia.........303
Winfield, Elias...................205
Winter & Cary.....................130
Winter, John...........129, 130, 131
Winthrop, _____ (Gov. of Mass.).115
Witherspoon, Dr. Jonathan. "The
    humble Confession, Declaration,
    Recantation and Apology of
    Benjamin Towne,"..............62
Wochentliche Philadelphische Staats-
    bote, Der, Philadelphia,Pa.....60
Wood, _____ 367
Wood & Crossfield.................273
Wood & White......................273
Wood, John.....................272-73
Woods, John..................189, 236
Woods's Newark Gazette, Newark,
    New Jersey...................236
Woodward, Augustus B. Considera-
    tions on the Executive Govern-
    ment of the United States.....219
    _____. Considerations on the
    Government of the Territory
    of Columbia..................270
    _____. Considerations on the
    Substance of the Sun.........271
    _____. Epaminondas on the Gov-
    ernment of the Territory of
    Columbia.... 270
Woolhopter, Philip D..............395
Workman, Samuel....................97
Worsley, William W................294
Worthington, Erastus...........217-18

Wortmann, Conrad...................80
Wright & Wilbur...................211
Wright, Goodenow & Stockwell......211
Wright, James (Ga. Gov.)..367-68, 370
                        378, 380, 390, 392
Wright, John C....................211
Wright, Wilbur & Stockwell........211
Wroth, Laurence C...99, 280, 284, 310
    _____. History of Printing in
    Colonial Maryland............99
Wyckoff & Brokaw..................208
Wyckoff, Cornelius P..............208
Wyeth, George......................98

York & Albany, Duke of............170
York Recorder, York, Pa............86
Young & Faust.....................335
Young, Edward.....................374
Young Ladies' and Gentlemen's
    Spelling Book, by Caleb
    Alexander....................193
Young Misses Magazine, The,
    Brooklyn, New York...........215
Young, William P..................335
Yundt & Brown.....................127
Yundt & Patton....................126
Yundt, Leonard.................126-27

Zeissiger, J. Georg................77
Zenger, John......................148
Zenger, John Peter.8, 107-8, 124, 138
                                140-48
    _____, wife............144, 148
Zionitischer Weyrauchs Hugel.......70
Zschokke, _____. Abaellino, the
    Bravo of Venice..............214
    _____. Aballino der Grosse
    Bandit.......................214
Zubly, John Joachim...............318

BIBLIOGRAPHY

BIBLIOGRAPHY

Adams, James Truslow. History of the Town of Southampton East of Canoe Place. (Bridgehampton, L. I., 1918).

Aikman, Mrs. Louisa Susannah (Wells). The Journal of a Voyage from Charleston, S.C., to London . . . in the year 1778. (New York, 1906).

Anderson, George Baker. Landmarks of Rensselaer County, New York. (Syracuse, 1897).

_____. Our County and People; a Descriptive and Biographical Record of Saratoga County, New York. (Boston, 1899).

Andrews, J. Cutler. "The Pittsburgh Gazette--a Pioneer Newspaper," Western Pennsylvania Magazine of History. v. 15, no. 4, November, 1932, p.293-307.

Arthur, John Preston. Western North Carolina. (Raleigh, 1914).

"Articles of Agreement between Benjamin Franklin and Lewis Timothee, 1733," Pennsylvania Magazine of History and Biography, v. 30, 1906, p. 104-106.

Atkinson, Joseph. The History of Newark. (Newark, 1878).

Bartlett, Elisha, M.D. A Brief Sketch of the Life, Character, and Writings of William Charles Wells, M.D., F.R.S. (Louisville, Ky., 1849).

Bausman, Lottie M. A Bibliography of Lancaster County, Pennsylvania, 1745-1912. (Philadelphia, 1912).

Benedict, William R. "James Parker, the Printer of Woodbridge," Proceedings of the New Jersey Historical Society, v. 8, 1923, p. 194-199.

Benton, Joel. "Some Early Hudson River Imprints," Literary Collector, v. 3, 1901-1902, p. 119-122.

"Bibliography of Virginia and West Virginia Legal Publications in Library of the College of Law, West Virginia University," West Virginia Law Quarterly, v. 26, November, 1919, p. 43-57.

Bloore, Stephen. "Samuel Keimer, a Footnote to the Life of Benjamin Franklin," Pennsylvania Magazine of History, v. 54, July, 1930, p. 255-287.

Boardman, George Dana. "Early Printing in the Middle Colonies," Pennsylvania Magazine of History, v. 10, 1886, p. 15-32.

Boyd, William Kenneth. History of North Carolina. (Chicago, 1919).

Boyd, William Kenneth. <u>Some</u> <u>Eighteenth</u> <u>Century</u> <u>Tracts</u> <u>Concerning</u> <u>North</u> <u>Carolina</u>. (Raleigh, 1927).

Boyer, Charles S. <u>History</u> <u>of</u> <u>the</u> <u>Press</u> <u>in</u> <u>Camden</u> <u>County</u>, <u>New</u> <u>Jersey</u>. (Camden, ca. 1920).

/¯ Bradford, William ¯/. <u>William</u> <u>Bradford</u>, <u>His</u> <u>Connection</u> <u>with</u> <u>Early</u> <u>Printing</u>; a sketch delivered at a meeting of the New York Historical Society subsequent to the placing of a tablet at the Hanover Square corner of the Cotton Exchange, (New York, n.d.).

Brigham, Clarence S. "Bibliography of American Newspapers, 1690-1820," <u>Proceed-ings</u> <u>of</u> <u>the</u> <u>American</u> <u>Antiquarian</u> <u>Society</u>, v. 23, 1913, p. 331-368, 370-394; v. 25, 1915, p. 128-192; v. 26, 1916, p. 413-460; v. 27, 1917, p. 177-274, 375-513; v. 28, 1918, p. 63-133, 291-322; v. 30, 1920, p. 81-150; v. 32, 1922, p. 81-214, 346-379; v. 34, 1924, p. 261-300; v. 37, 1927, p. 63-155.

_____. "Franklin's German Newspaper, 1751-52," <u>Proceedings</u> <u>of</u> <u>the</u> <u>Mass-achusetts</u> <u>Historical</u> <u>Society</u>. v. 56, 1922-23, p. 301-305.

Brumbaugh, Martin G. "Life and Work of Bishop Christopher Sower," in <u>Bishop</u> <u>Christopher</u> <u>Sower</u> <u>of</u> <u>Germantown</u>. <u>Memorial</u> <u>Services</u>. <u>Presentation</u> <u>of</u> <u>Tablet</u>. <u>Church</u> <u>of</u> <u>The</u> <u>Brethren</u>, <u>Germantown</u>, <u>January</u> <u>1</u>, <u>1899</u>. (Germantown, 1899 /?_/).

Bryan, Wilhelmus Bogart. <u>Bibliography</u> <u>of</u> <u>the</u> <u>District</u> <u>of</u> <u>Columbia</u> . . . <u>to</u> <u>1898</u>. (Washington, 1900.)

_____. <u>A</u> <u>History</u> <u>of</u> <u>the</u> <u>National</u> <u>Capital</u>, v. I, (New York, 1914).

"Brynberg, the Printer," <u>Literary</u> <u>Collector</u>, v. 1, no. 4, 1900, p. 25-26.

Bullen, Henry Lewis. "Famous American Printers, No. 2--Mathew Carey," <u>Ameri-can</u> <u>Collector</u>, v. 1, no. 3, December, 1925, p. 86-92.

_____. "Famous American Printers, No. 3--The Bradford Family of Printers," <u>American</u> <u>Collector</u>, v. 1, no. 4, January, 1926, p. 148-156, 164-170.

_____. "The Oldest Job Printing Office in New York," <u>Inland</u> <u>Printer</u>, v. 50, 1913, p. 519-521.

Campbell, William J. <u>The</u> <u>Collection</u> <u>of</u> <u>Franklin</u> <u>Imprints</u> <u>in</u> <u>the</u> <u>Museum</u> <u>of</u> <u>the</u> <u>Curtis</u> <u>Publishing</u> <u>Company</u>. (Philadelphia, 1918).

_____. "Unknown Issues of the Journals of the Continental Congress," <u>American</u> <u>Collector</u>, v. 3, no. 3, December, 1926, p. 114-118.

Carter, W. C., and A. J. Glossbrenner. <u>History</u> <u>of</u> <u>York</u> <u>County</u> <u>from</u> <u>its</u> <u>Erection</u> <u>to</u> <u>the</u> <u>Present</u> <u>Time</u> /¯ 1729-1834 ¯/. New edition; with additions edited by A. Monroe Aurand, Jr. (Harrisburg, 1930).

Clark, Allen C. "Daniel Rapine, the Second Mayor," Records of the Columbia Historical Society, v. 25, 1923, p. 194.

_____. "Joseph Gales, Junior, Editor and Mayor," Records of the Columbia Historical Society, v. 23, 1920, p. 86-145.

Clayton-Torrence, William. "A Trial Bibliography of Colonial Virginia," appended to Fifth Annual Report of the Library Board of the Virginia State Library, 1907-1908, p. 1-154.

_____. "A Trial Bibliography of Colonial Virginia (1754-1776)," appended to Sixth Annual Report of the Library Board of the Virginia State Library, 1908-1909. p. 1-94.

Clearwater, Alphonso Trumpbour. History of Ulster County, New York. (Kingston, 1907).

Collins, Varnum Lansing. Early Princeton Printing. (Princeton, 1911).

"Colonial Printers in New York," Book Buyer, n.s., v. 13, February, 1896, p. 8-10.

Conrad, Henry C. History of the State of Delaware (Wilmington, Delaware, 1908). v. 3.

_____. "The Press of Delaware," in L.P. Powell, History of Education in Delaware. (Washington, 1893), p. 178-186.

Corbitt, D. L. "The North Carolina Gazette," North Carolina Historical Review, v. 2, 1925, p. 83-86.

Craig, Neville B. The History of Pittsburgh. (Pittsburgh, 1851).

Creigh, Alfred. History of Washington County. (Washington, Pa., 1870)

Crittenden, Charles Christopher. North Carolina Newspapers Before 1790. (Chapel Hill, N. Car., 1928) (James Sprunt Historical Studies, v. 20, no. 1).

Cundall, Frank. "The Press and Printers of Jamaica to 1820," Proceedings of the American Antiquarian Society, v. 26, 1916, p. 290-412. (Also issued in pamphlet form, 1916.)

Curry, Henry B. "New York Journalism's 200 Years," New York Herald-Tribune, November 1, 1925, Section 7, p. 1-2.

Dahlinger, Charles William. Pittsburgh: A Sketch of Its Early Social Life. (New York, 1916).

Dapp, Charles Frederick. The Evolution of an American Patriot . . . John Henry Miller. (Philadelphia, 1924). (Reprinted from Proceedings of the Pennsylvania German Society, v. 32).

_____. "Johann Heinrich Miller," German-American Annals, n.s., v. 14, 1916, p. 118-136.

Dearden, Robert R., Jr., and Douglas C. Watson. The Bible of the Revolution. (San Fransicso, 1931).

Diffenderffer, Frank Reid. "Early German Printers of Lancaster and the Issues of their Press," Proceedings of the Lancaster Historical Society, v. 8, no. 3, 1904.

_____. "An Early Newspaper," Lancaster County Historical Papers, v. 11, 1907, p. 175-194.

_____. The Oldest Daily Paper in Lancaster County. (Lancaster, 1896).

"Domestic Piety and Religion," Pennsylvania German Society Proceedings, v. 10, 1900, p. 38-52.

Eames, Wilberforce. "The Antigua Press and Benjamin Mecom," Proceedings of the American Antiquarian Society, v. 38, 1928, p. 303-348.

_____. "The First American Edition of Wither's Poems and Bacon's Essays," The Bibliographer, v. 1, 1902, p. 11-21.

Eddy, George Simpson, ed. Account Books Kept by Benjamin Franklin (1728-1747). (New York, 1928 and 1929). 2 v.

_____. A Work-Book of the Printing House of Benjamin Franklin & David Hall, 1759-1766. (New York, 1930). (Reprinted from the Bulletin of the New York Public Library, August, 1930).

Ellis, Franklin. History of Columbia County, New York. (Philadelphia, 1878).

_____, and Samuel Evans. History of Lancaster County, Pennsylvania. (Philadelphia, 1883).

Evans, Charles. American Bibliography. (Chicago, 1903-34). v. 1-12.

"Extracts from the First Georgia Newspaper-- The Gazette," Georgia Historical Quarterly, v. 1, 1917. p. 49-51.

Fauteux, Aegidius. "Fleury Mesplet: une Etude sur les Commecements de l'Imprimerie dans la Ville de Montreal," Papers of the Bibliographical Society of America, v. 28, 1934, p. 164-193.

Fauteux, Aegidius. The Introduction of Printing into Canada. (Montreal, 1930).

Faÿ, Bernard. Franklin, the Apostle of Modern Times. (Boston, 1929).

"The First German Newspaper Published in America," Pennsylvania Magazine of History, v. 24, 1900, p. 306-307.

"The First School Book Printed in Virginia," Pennsylvania-German, v. 12, 1911, p. 300-301.

Follett, Frederick. History of the Press in Western New York from the Beginning to the Middle of the Nineteenth Century, (Heartman Reprint), (New York, 1920).

Force, Peter. American Archives. Washington, D.C., Series 4, v. 3, columns 847, 923, 1031; Series 4, v. 4, column 540.

Ford, Paul Leicester. "The Battle of Brooklyn," The Bibliographer. v. 1, 1902, p. 69-71.

_____. "The Crisis," The Bibliographer, v. 1, 1902, p. 139-152, 195.

_____. "Donkin's Military Collections," The Bibliographer, v. 1, 1902, p. 22-26.

_____. The Journals of Hugh Gaine, Printer. (New York, 1902). 2 v.

Ford, Worthington Chauncey. "Franklin's Advice to a Young Tradesman; two unique impressions," The Bibliographer, v. 1, 1902, p. 89-96.

_____, ed. /_ Letters from and concerning James Parker to Benjamin Franklin, 1741-1773_/, Proceedings of the Massachusetts Historical Society, 2nd series, v. 16, 1903, p. 186-231.

Forrest, Earle R. History of Washington County, Pennsylvania. (Chicago, 1926). v. 1

Fowler, Robert Ludlow. Facsimile of the Laws and Acts of the General Assembly . . . of New York . . . William Bradford . . . 1694. (New York, 1894).

French, Alvah P. "Early History of Westchester County Newspapers," Americana, v. 18, 1924, p. 102-104.

Frick, Bertha Margaret. A History of Printing in Virginia, 1750-1783, with a list of Virginia imprints for that period. Unpublished master's thesis, Graduate School of Library Science, Columbia University, 1933.

Geist, J. M. W. "Newspapers in Lancaster County," in J. I. Mombert's Authentic History of Lancaster County. (Lancaster, 1896).

Gibson, James. "Journalism in Salem," in /¯Crisfield Johnson_7. History of Washington County, New York. (Philadelphia, 1878).

Greely, A W. Public Documents of the First Fourteen Congresses, 1789-1817. (Washington, 1900).

Green, Henry S. "Early Newspapers in the Virginias," Ohio Archaeological and Historical Quarterly, v. 25, 1916, p. 190-202.

Griffin, A. P. C. "Issue of the District of Columbia Press in 1800-02," Records of the Columbia Historical Society, v. 4, 1901, p. 32-74.

Grolier Club. Catalogue of Books Printed by William Bradford. (New York, 1892).

Grose, Edward F. Centennial History of the Village of Ballston Spa. (Ballston, 1907).

/¯Grose, H. L._7. "The Press of Saratoga," in Nathaniel Bartlett Sylvester. History of Saratoga County, New York. (Philadelphia, 1878).

Halsey, Francis Whiting. "The Beginnings of Daily Journalism in New York City," New York State Historical Association Proceedings, v. 17, 1919, p. 87-99.

_____. "Journalism in New York in 1800," Journalist. April 7, 1900.

Harbaugh, Linn. "Introductory /¯sic_7 to Bibliography of Franklin County," Kittochtinny Historical Society Papers, v. 7, 1912, p. 90-99.

Harden, William. "Savannah Newspapers," in his History of Savannah and South Georgia. (Chicago and New York, 1913). v. 1, p. 513-515.

Harvey, Oscar J. "Wilkes-Barre's Earliest Newspapers," Proceedings of the Wyoming Historical and Geological Society, v. 18, p. 59-98.

Hasse, Adelaide R. "Bayard's Journal, the First Book Printed in New York," Bibliographer, v. 2, March, 1903, p. 189-195.

_____. "The First Published Proceedings of an American Legislature," The Bibliographer, v. 2, 1903, p. 240-242.

_____. "New York in 1696; a note to accompany the proclamation of September 12, 1696." Literary Collector, v. 6, no. 5, September, 1903, p. 138-142.

_____. Some Materials for a Bibliography of the Official Publications of the General Assembly of the Colony of New York, 1693-1775. (Reprinted from the Bulletin of the New York Public Library, February-April, 1903).

Hawkins, Dorothy Lawson. "James Adams, the First Printer of Delaware," Papers of the Bibliographical Society of America, v. 28, part I, 1934, p. 28-63.

Heartman, Charles F. A Bibliography of the Writings of Hugh Henry Brackenridge, prior to 1825. (New York, 1917).

_____. John Peter Zenger and His Fight for the Freedom of the American Press. (Highland Park, N.J., 1934).

/ Heartman, Charles F. / Preliminary Checklist of Almanacs Printed in New Jersey Prior to 1850. (Metuchen, N.J., 1930).

Hildeburn, Charles R. A Century of Printing. The Issues of the Press of Pennsylvania, 1685-1784. 2v. (Philadelphia, 1885).

Supplements to Hildeburn's Century of Printing have been prepared as theses in the Graduate School of Library Science of Columbia University: for the period 1685-1775 by Ethel Myra Metzger (1930) and for 1776-1784 by Edith Stevens Taylor (1935); both theses are still in manuscript.

/ Hildeburn, Charles R. / The Charlemagne Tower Collection of Early Colonial Laws. (Philadelphia, 1890).

_____. "A List of the Issues of the Press in New York, 1693-1720," Pennsylvania Magazine of History and Biography, v. 12, 1889, p. 475-482.

_____. A List of the Issues of the Press in New York, 1693-1752. (Philadelphia, 1889).

_____. "Printing in New York in the Seventeenth Century," American History Magazine, v. 8, 1908, p. 297-308. (Reprinted? from J. G. Wilson, Memorial History of the City of New York. New York, 1892. v. 1, p. 570-603.)

_____. Sketches of Printers and Printing in Colonial New York. (New York, 1895).

Hill, Frank P., and Varnum L. Collins. Books, Pamphlets and Newspapers Printed at Newark, New Jersey, 1776-1900. (Newark, 1902).

Hill, William H. A Brief History of the Printing Press in Washington, Saratoga, and Warren Counties, New York. (Fort Edward, N.Y., 1930).

Holden, William Woods. Address of the History of Journalism in North Carolina. (Raleigh, 1881).

Hornor, W. M., Jr. "The First Directory of New York, as Compiled by David Franks in 1786," American Collector, v. 2, no. 6, September, 1926, p. 452-461.

Hornor, W. M., Jr. "Notes Concerning the . . . Publication of the Saur Bible," American Collector, v. 5, 1927, p. 60-68.

Howell, George Rogers, and others. Bi-Centennial History of Albany. (New York, 1886).

_____ and John H. Munsell, editors. History of the County of Schenectady, New York, from 1662 to 1886. (New York, 1886).

/ Hoyt, Albert Harrison /. "Early Printing in Virginia," New England Historical and Genealogical Register, v. 26, 1872, p. 30-36.

Huch, C. F. von. "Die erste deutsche Zeitung in Philadelphia," Mitteilungen des Deutschen Pionier Vereins von Philadelphia, 7th pt, 1908, p. 20-27; and 8th pt., 1908, p. 29-32.

Humphrey, Constance H. "Check-List of New Jersey Imprints to the End of the Revolution," Papers of the Bibliographical Society of America, v. 24, 1930, p. 43-149.

Hutchinson, Elmer T. "A Forgotten Elizabethtown Newspaper, the Essex Patriot," Proceedings of the New Jersey Historical Society, v. 8, 1923, p. 210-219.

"Introduction of Printing into New York," Publishers' Weekly, v. 35, 1889, p. 665-666.

Johnson, A. L. "Career of Journal Started in Darkest Days of Revolution," Elizabeth Daily Journal, 150th anniversary edition, February 16, 1929, p. 2-4. See also p. 9.

Johnson, Crisfield. History of Washington County, New York. (Philadelphia, 1878).

Johnson, Maud E. "A Bibliography of New Jersey Bibliographies," Proceedings of the New Jersey Historical Society, 3d series, v. 10, 1915, p. 61-62.

Jones, Charles C., Jr. Memorial History of Augusta, Georgia, from Its Settlement in 1735 to the Close of the 18th Century. (Syracuse, N.Y., 1890). Chapter XXV, "The Press," p. 278-290.

Jones Horatio Gates. An Address Delivered February 9th, 1869 . . . Andrew Bradford, founder of the newspaper press in the middle states of America. (Philadelphia, 1869.)

/ Jones, Horatio Gates /. The Bradford Prayer Book, 1710. Some account of the Book of Common Prayer, printed . . . by William Bradford, under the auspices of Trinity Church, New York. (Philadelphia, 1870).

_____. "The First Book Ever Printed in Philadelphia," Historical Magazine, v. 8, 1864, p. 274-276.

Jordan, John W. "Rev. John Brandmiller, the Moravian Printer," _Pennsylvania Magazine of History_, v. 6, 1882, p. 249-250.

Jorgenson, Chester E. "A Brand Flung at Colonial Orthodoxy," _Journalism Quarterly_, v. 12, no. 3, September, 1935, p. 272-277.

Keidel, George C. _The Earliest German Newspapers of Baltimore_. (Washington, 1927).

Kent, Henry W. "Chez Moreau de st-Mery, Philadelphia," in _Bibliographical Essays, a Tribute to Wilberforce Eames_. (Cambridge, Mass., 1924).

Kerr, R. W. _History of the Government Printing Office_, a record of public printing for the century 1789 to 1881. (Lancaster, 1881).

Killikelly, Sarah H. _History of Pittsburgh_. (Pittsburgh, 1906).

King, Marion Reynolds. "One Link in the First Newspaper Chain, The South Carolina Gazette," _Journalism Quarterly_, v. 9, 1932, p. 257-268.

King, William L. _The Newspaper Press of Charleston, S. C._ (Charleston, S.C., 1882).

Kite, Nathan. _Researches Among the Early Printers and Publishers of Friends' Books_. (Manchester, England, 1844). (Reprinted from "Antiquarian Researches," in The Friend, v. 16, 1843, p. 373-374, 379-380, 392, 397, 406-407, 415; v. 17, 1843, p. 12-13, 21-22, 28-29, 44-45, 54.).

Klock, Jay E. "The Newspapers of Ulster," in Alphonso Trumpbour Clearwater, _History of Ulster County, New York_. (Kingston, 1907).

Knauss, James Owen. "Christopher Saur the Third," _Proceedings of the American Antiquarian Society_, v. 41, 1931, p. 235-253.

_____. _Social Conditions Among the Pennsylvania Germans in the Eighteenth Century_ as revealed in the German newspapers published in America. (Lancaster, 1922).

Kollock, Shepard, III. /¯Memoirs of his grandfather¯_/, _Elizabeth Daily Journal_, 150th anniversary edition, February 16, 1929, p. 10 and 23.

Leach, M. Atherton. "Zachariah Poulson," _American-Scandinavian Review_, v. 8, 1920, p. 510-517.

Lee, Alfred McClung. "Dunlap and Claypoole: Printers and News-Merchants of the Revolution," _Journalism Quarterly_, v. 11, no. 2, 1934, p. 160-178.

_____. "First U.S. Daily 50 Years Too Early," _Editor & Publisher_, v. 66, no. 44, March 17, 1934, p. 12, 40.

Lee, Alfred McClung. "The Pioneer American Daily in 1783," Editor & Publisher, v. 66, no. 43, March 10, 1934, p. 11, 37.

Lee, John Thomas. "The First Edition of the Zenger Trial, 1736," Wisconsin Magazine of History, v. 1, 1917, p. 69-72.

Letters of Benjmain Franklin and his son William Franklin to William Strahan, the Publisher. (Philadelphia, 1905).

/ Lingard, Richard /. "The First Book Printed in New York," Journal of American History, v. 3, 1909, p. 265, 274.

Lyon, James B. The Lyon Family. (Jacksonville, Florida, 1923).

Mackall, Leonard L. "First Book Printed in South Carolina," New York Herald Tribune Books, March 13, 1932, p. 19.

_____. "William Parks, Printer in England and America, 1719-49," in "Notes for Bibliographers," New York Herald Tribune Books, May 15, 1927.

/ Mackall, Leonard L. and Azalea Clizbee /. Catalogue of the Wymberley Jones DeRenne Georgia Library at Wormsloe, Isle of Hope, near Savannah, Georgia. 3 volumes. (Wormsloe, privately printed, 1930).

Markland, J. Typographia: An Ode on Printing. (Roanoke, Va., 1926). / Facsimile of 1730 edition, with Introduction by E. G. Swem, produced by the eminent Virginia printer, Edward L. Stone /.

Martin, Charlotte M., and Benjamin Ellis. The New York Press and Its Makers in the Eighteenth Century. (New York, 1898).

"A Masterpiece of American Colonial Printing," Chicago Historical Society Bulletin, v. 1, no. 3, September, 1922, p. 22-24.

On the Chicago Historical Society's copy of Der Blutige Schau-Platz, oder Martyrer Spiegel, Ephrata, 1748.

Mease, James. Picture of Philadelphia (Philadelphia, 1831).

Memoirs of W. C. Wells . . . With an account of his writings. (London, 1818). Extracted from the Gentleman's Magazine, Oct. and Nov., 1817.

Miller, Daniel. "Early German American Newspapers," Proceedings of the Pennsylvania German Society, 1908, v. 19. 1910. / sic /.

_____. "The German Newspapers of Berks County," Berks County Historical Society Transactions, v. 3, 1912, p. 4-22.

Miller, Daniel. "The German Newspapers of Lebanon County," Lebanon County Historical Society Papers, v. 5, no. 4, 1910.

Mitchell, Edward Page. "Colonial Journalism in New York," Proceedings of the New York State Historical Society, v. 16, 1917, p. 120-136.

Mombert, J. I. An Authentic History of Lancaster County. (Lancaster, Pa., 1869).

Monroe, Joel Henry. Schenectady, Ancient and Modern. (Geneva, 914 /̄ i.e. 1914? /̄).

Moore, George Henry. Historical Notes on the Introduction of Printing into New York. (New York, 1888).

Mori, Gustav. "Der Buchdrucker Christoph Saur in Germantown," Gutenberg Jahrbuch, (Mainz, 1934).

_____. Die Egenolff-Luthersche Schriftgiesserei in Frankfurt am Main und ihre geschaftlichen Verbindungen mit den Vereinigten Staaten von Nordamerika. (Frankfurt am Main, 1926).

Morrell, E. "Librorum Rarissima," Stone's Impressions, n. s vol. 3, no. 3, May-June, 1933, p. 8-9.

Morsch, Lucile M. A Checklist of New Jersey Imprints, 1784-1800; with an introductory essay on the history of printing in New Jersey during this period. Unpublished master's thesis, Graduate School of Library Science, Columbia University, 1930.

Mott, Frank Luther. A History of American Magazines, 1741-1850. (New York and London, 1930).

Munsell, Joel. Typographical Miscellany. (Albany, 1850).

McClellan, William J. /̄ Articles on the Goddards at Baltimore /̄, Baltimore American, August 20, 1898, August 17, 1902, and August 27, 1905.

McClure, A. K. "Pennsylvania Journalism," in Pennsylvania Colonial and Federal. (Philadelphia, 1903).

McCombs, Charles F. "John Peter Zenger, Printer," Bulletin of the New York Public Library, v. 37, no. 12, p. 1031-1034.

McCreary, George W. The First Book Printed in Baltimore-Town, Nicholas Hasselbach, Printer. (Baltimore, 1903).

McCulloch, William, "Additions to Thomas's History of Printing," Proceedings of the American Antiquarian Society, v. 31, 1921, p. 89-247.

McMaster, John Bach. Benjamin Franklin as a Man of Letters. (London, 1887).

McMurtrie, Douglas Crawford. "The Beginnings of Printing in the District of Columbia," _Americana,_ v. 27, no. 3, July, 1933, p. 265-289.

_____. _The Beginnings of Printing in Virginia._ (Lexington, Virginia, 1935).

_____. _Benjamin Franklin, Typefounder._ (New York, 1925).

_____. "A Bibliography of Morristown Imprints, 1798-1820," _Proceedings of the New Jersey Historical Society,_ v. 54, no. 2, April, 1936, p. 129-155.

_____. "A Bibliography of North Carolina Imprints, 1761-1800," _North Carolina Historical Review,_ v. 13, no. 1, January, 1936, p. 47-86, and subsequent issues.

_____. "A Bibliography of South Carolina Imprints, 1731-1740," _South Carolina Historical and Genealogical Magazine,_ v. 34, no. 3, July 1, 1933, p. 117-137.

_____. "The Correspondence of Peter Timothy, Printer of Charlestown, with Benjamin Franklin," _South Carolina Historical and Genealogical Magazine,_ v. 35, no. 4, October, 1934, p. 123-129.

_____. "The Delaware Imprints of 1761," _American Book Collector,_ v. 2, nos. 2-3, August-September, 1932, p. 135-137.

_____. "The Earliest New Jersey Imprint," _Proceedings of the New Jersey Historical Society,_ v. 50, no. 2, April, 1932, p. 191-202.

_____. _Early Printing in Kentucky, with a bibliography of the issues of the press, 1787-1830._ (In manuscript.)

_____. _Early Printing in Pittsburgh, with a bibliography of the issues of the press, 1786-1830._ (In manuscript.)

_____. _Editorial note on a Maryland broadside of 1737._ _Ars Typographica,_ v. 2, no. 4, April, 1916, p. 317-318.

_____. "The First Decade of Printing in the Royal Province of South Carolina," _Transactions of the Bibliographical Society,_ n.s., v. 13, no. 4, March, 1933, p. 425-452.

_____. _The First Printing in Georgia._ (Metuchen, N.J., printed for Charles Heartman, 1927.)

_____. _The First Twelve Years of Printing in North Carolina, 1749-1760._ (Raleigh, 1933) (Reprinted from _North Carolina Historical Review,_ v. 10, no. 3, July, 1933, p. 214-234.)

_____. _Four South Carolina Imprints of 1731, together with complete facsimiles of these imprints._ (Chicago, 1933).

Nichols, L. Nelson. "In Georgia," American Printer. v. 86, no. 4, January, 1928, p. 74-75.

_____. "Printing in New York State," American Printer, v. 81, November, 1925, p. 42.

_____. "Studies in Early American Imprints: New Jersey," American Printer, v. 81, December, 1925, p. 42.

_____. "Studies in Early American Imprints: Pennsylvania," American Printer, v. 82, January, 1926, p. 49-50.

Nolan, J. Bennett. The First Decade of Printing in Reading, Pennsylvania. (Reading, 1930).

Nutt, John J. Newburgh, Her Institutions, Industries and Leading Citizens.

"Old Virginia Editors," William and Mary College Quarterly, v. 7, 1899.

Oswald, John Clyde. Benjamin Franklin, Printer. (Garden City, N.Y., 1917).

_____. "Francis Childs and New York's First Daily," National Printer Journalist, v. 50, no. 2, February, 1932, p. 14-15.

Paltsits, Victor Hugo. "Almanacs of Roger Sherman, 1750 to 1761," Proceedings of the American Antiquarian Society, v. 18, 1906-1907, p. 213-258

_____. A Bibliography of the Separate and Collected Works of Philip Freneau. (New York, 1903).

_____. "John Holt--Printer and Postmaster," Bulletin of the New York Public Library, v. 24, no. 9, September, 1920, p. 483-499.

_____. "John Holt, Public Printer of New York, to the President of the Senate," Bulletin of the New York Public Library, v. 26, no. 10, October, 1922, p. 942-943.

_____. "Rare Factional Pamphlet, Printed at New York by James Parker in 1747," Literary Collector, v. 7, no. 1, November, 1903, p. 1-5.

Parker, Amasa Junius. Landmarks of Albany County, New York. (Syracuse, 1897).

Pattee, Fred Lewis. "Bibliography of Philip Freneau," The Bibliographer, v. 1, 1902, p. 97-106.

Pennypacker, Samuel W. "The Settlement of Germantown," Pennsylvania Magazine of History and Biography, v. 4, 1880, p. 1-41.

Pennypacker, Samuel W. "Sower and Beissel," in his Pennsylvania in American History (Philadelphia, 1910), p. 327-363. (Reprinted from Pennsylvania Magazine of History, v. 12, 1888, p. 76-96.

"Philadelphische Zeitung, the first German newspaper in America," Pennsylvania Magazine of History, v. 26, 1902, p. 91.

Phillips, Henry Jr. "Certain Almanacs Published in Philadelphia between 1705 and 1744," Proceedings of the American Philosophical Society, v. 19, 1882, p. 291-297.

Poore, Ben Perley. A Descriptive Catalogue of the Government Publications of the United States, 1774-1881. (Washington, 1885).

"Post Offices and Newspapers in New Jersey in 1811," Proceedings of the New Jersey Historical Society, n. s., v. 10, p. 175-176.

Powell, Walter A. A History of Delaware. (Boston, 1928).

Purple, Samuel S. Bradford Family. (New York, 1931).

Richards, Louis. "The First Newspaper in Pennsylvania," Berks County Historical Society Transactions, v. 2, 1910, p. 335-358.

Richardson, Lyon N. A History of Early American Magazines, 1741-1789. (New York, 1931).

Riley, Elihu S. The Ancient City; a History of Annapolis in Maryland, 1649-1887. (Annapolis, 1887).

Ritenour, John S. "Early Newspapers of Southwestern Pennsylvania," Inland Printer, v. 51, 1913, p. 427-430.

Robinson, William Erigena. "The History of the Press of Brooklyn and Kings County . . ." in Henry R. Stiles. Civil, Political Professional and Ecclesiastical History of . . . Brooklyn, New York. (New York, 1884).

Rose, Grace D. "Early Morristown Imprints," Proceedings of the New Jersey Historical Society, v. 53, no. 3, July, 1935, p. 156-163.

Rosenbach, A. S. W. "William Bradford, the First Printer in the Middle Colonies."

    An address before the Historical Society of Pennsylvania on November 11, 1935; will probably be published in the Pennsylvania Magazine of History and Biography.

Rupp, I. Daniel. History of Lancaster and York Counties. (Lancaster, 1844).

Rutherfurd, Livingston. John Peter Zenger, His Press, His Trial, and a Bibliography of Zenger Imprints. (New York, 1904).

Ruttenber, Edward Manning and L. H. Clark. History of Orange County, New York. (Philadelphia, 1881).

_____. History of the Town of Newburgh. (Newburgh, 1859).

Sabine, Lorenzo. Biographical Sketches of Loyalists of the American Revolution. (Boston, 1864). 2v.

Sachse, Julius Friedrich. The German Sectarians of Pennsylvania, 1742-1800. (Philadelphia, 1899, 1900). 2v.

_____. "Reynier Jansen," in his German Pietists of Provincial Pennsylvania. (Philadelphia, 1895). p. 100-108.

Salley, A. S., Jr. "Contents of the South-Carolina Gazette, January, February, 1732," Gulf States Historical Magazine, v. 2, 1903-1904, p. 215-222.

_____. "The First Presses of South Carolina," Bibliographical Society of America Proceedings and Papers, v. 2, 1907-1908, p. 28-69.

Sargent, George H. "Additional Imprints of James Rivington," American Collector, v. 2, no. 5, August, 1926. p. 413-415.

_____. "Another 'Lost' Book Found," Publishers' Weekly, March 16, 1929, p. 1428-1430.

The "Unique first American edition of Robinson Crusoe," printed by Hugh Gaine in 1774.

_____. "A Bibliography of the Imprints of James Rivington," American Collector, v. 2, no. 4, July, 1926, p. 369-377.

_____. "James Rivington, the Tory Printer: A Study of the Loyalist Pamphlets of the Revolution," American Collector, v. 2, no. 3, June, 1926, p. 336-341.

Scharf, John Thomas. History of Delaware, 1609-1888. (Philadelphia, 1888). v.1.

_____, and Thompson Westcott. History of Philadelphia, 1609-1884. (Philadelphia, 1884).

/ Seaton, Josephine /. William Winston Seaton of the National Intelligencer. (Boston, 1871).

Seidensticker, Oswald. The First Century of German Printing in America, 1728-1830. (Philadelphia, 1893).

Shearer, Augustus Hunt. "Biographical and Descriptive Notes on the Issues of the Journal of the Pennsylvania Assembly, 1776-1790," Pennsylvania Magazine of History, v. 41, 1917, p. 359-364.

_____. "Le Courier de l'Amerique, Philadelphia, 1784," Papers of the Bibliographical Society of America, v. 14, 1920, p. 45-55.

Smith, H. Perry. History of Essex County, New York. (Syracuse, 1885).

Smith, James Hadden. History of Duchess County, New York. (Syracuse, 1882).

Smith, Joseph. Short Biographical Notices of William Bradford, Reiner Jansen, Andrew Bradford, and Samuel Keimer, Early Printers in Pennsylvania. (London, 1891).

Verbatim exerpt from Kite, with no further material included.

Smith, W. Roy. South Carolina as a Royal Province. (New York, 1903).

Smyth, Albert H. The Philadelphia Magazines and their Contributors, 1741-1850. (Philadelphia, 1892).

_____, editor. The Writings of Benjamin Franklin. (New York, 1905). 10v.

Sower, Charles G. "Presentation of a Tablet in memory of Christopher Sower, Father and Son, to the Church of the Brethren in Germantown, January 1, 1899," in Bishop Christopher Sower of Germantown. Memorial Services. Presentation of Tablet. Church of The Brethren, Germantown, January 1, 1899. (Germantown, 1899).

Stanard, W. G. "Books in Colonial Virginia," Nation, v. 88, 1909, p. 109-110.

Stiles, Henry R. Civil, Political, Professional and Ecclesiastical History of . . . Brooklyn, New York. (New York, 1884).

Stockbridge, Frank Parker. "Original Ulster Gazette is Found," The American Press, v. 49, no. 5, February, 1931, p. 1-3.

Stokes, I. N. Phelps. Iconography of Manhattan Island, 1498-1909. (6v. New York, 1928 et seq.). v.2

Stone, W. L. "Early History of the Printing and Newspaper Press in Boston and New York," Continental Monthly, v. 4, 1863, p. 257-268.

Stone, W. L. Washington County, New York; Its History to the Close of the Nineteenth Century. (New York, 1901).

Stoudt, John Joseph. "The German Press in Pennsylvania and the American Revolution," Pennsylvania Magazine of History, v. 59, no. 253, January, 1935, p. 74-90.

Swain, David L. "The British Invasion of North Carolina in 1776," North Carolina University Magazine, v. 2, 1853, p. 147-148.

Swem, Earl G. "A Bibliography of Virginia. Part I. Containing the Titles of Books in the Virginia State Library Which Relate to Virginia and Virginians . . . but not including the titles of . . . published official documents," Bulletin of the Virginia State Library, v. 8, 1915, p. 35-767.

_____. "A Bibliography of Virginia. Part II. Containing titles of the printed official documents of the Commonwealth, 1776-1916," Bulletin of the Virginia State Library, v. 10, 1917, p. 1-1404.

_____. "A Bibliography of Virginia. Part III. Containing the acts and the journals of the General Assembly of the colony, 1619-1776," Bulletin of the Virginia State Library, v. 12, 1919, p. 1-71.

_____. / Introduction to / Typographia: An Ode on Printing, reissued in photographic facsimile from Williamsburg edition of 1730. (Roanoke, 1926).

Sylvester, Nathaniel Bartlett. History of Rensselaer County, New York. (Philadelphia, 1880).

_____. History of Saratoga County, New York. (Philadelphia, 1878).

_____. History of Ulster County, New York. (Philadelphia, 1880).

Tapley, Harriet Silvester. Salem Imprints, 1768-1825. (Salem, Mass., 1927).

Tenney, Jonathan. "Journalists and Journalism in Albany County," in George Rogers Howell and others, Bi-Centennial History of Albany. (New York, 1886).

Thomas, Charles M. "John Holt, Printer of the Revolution," American Press, v. 51, no. 10, July, 1933, p. 16.

_____. "The Publication of Newspapers during the American Revolution," Journalism Quarterly, v. 9, no. 4, December, 1932, p. 358-373.

Thomas, Isaiah. The History of Printing in America. Second Edition. (Albany, 1874). 2v.

Thompson, Benjamin F. History of Long Island from Its Discovery and Settlement to the Present Time. Third edition. (New York, 1918). 4v.

Thurston, George H. Allegheny County's Hundred Years. (Pittsburgh, 1888).

Thwaites, Reuben Gold. "The Ohio Valley Press Before the War of 1812-15," Proceedings of the American Antiquarian Society, v. 19, 1908-1909, p. 309-368, at 310-319.

Tinker, Edward Larocque. "Jurist and Japer, Francois Xavier Martin and Jean Leclerc with a list of their publications . . ." Bulletin of the New York Public Library, v. 39, no. 9, September, 1935, p. 675-697.

Tooker, William Wallace. "Early Sag-Harbor Printers and Their Imprints," Sag Harbor Express, January, 1902.

Vail, R. W. G. "The Ulster County Gazette and Its Illegitimate Offspring," Bulletin of the New York Public Library, v. 34, no. 4, April, 1930, p. 207-238.

_____. "The Ulster County Gazette Found at Last," Bulletin of the New York Public Library, v. 35, no. 4, April, 1931, p. 207-211.

Wall, Alexander J. "The Burning of the Pamphlet, 'The Deceiver Unmasked' in 1776," American Collector, v. 3, no. 3, December, 1926, p. 106-111.

_____. A List of New York Almanacs. (New York, 1920). (Reprinted from Bulletin of the New York Public Library, v. 24, May-November, 1920).

_____. "Samuel Loudon (1727-1813), Merchant, Printer and Patriot, with some of his letters," New York Historical Society Quarterly Bulletin, v. 6, October, 1922, p. 75-92.

Wallace, John William. / Bradford Bicentennial Address / An Address delivered at the celebration by the New York Historical Society, May 20, 1863, of the two hundredth birth day of Mr. William Bradford, who introduced the art of printing into the middle colonies of British America. (Albany, 1863).

_____. "Early Printing in Philadelphia. The Friends Press--Interregnum of the Bradfords," Pennsylvania Magazine of History, v. 4, 1880, p. 432-444.

Warden, D. B. Chorographical Description of the District of Columbia. (Paris, 1816).

Warrington, James. "A Bibliography of Church Music Books Issued in Pennsylvania, with Annotations," Pennsylvania Germania, n.s., v. 1, 1912, p. 170-177, 262-268.

Watt, S. F. "Bergen County Bibliography," Bergen County Historical Society Papers, v. 11, 1916, p. 115-117.

Webber, Mable L. "South Carolina Almanacs, to 1800," South Carolina Historical Magazine, v. 25, 1914, p. 73-81.

/ Weeks, Stephen Beauregard_/. "The Earliest Newspapers of North Carolina," Magazine of American History, v. 22, 1889, p. 429-430.

Weeks, Stephen Beauregard. "Libraries and Literature in North Carolina in the Eighteenth Century," Annual Report of the American Historical Association for 1895. (Washington, 1896). p. 171-267.

With a supplement to the list of publications in his Press of North Carolina.

_____. "The Pre-Revolutionary Printers of North Carolina: Davis, Steuart, and Boyd," North Carolina Booklet, v. 15, 1915, p. 104-121.

_____. The Press of North Carolina in the Eighteenth Century. (Brooklyn, 1891).

Wegelin, Oscar. Books Relating to the History of Georgia in the Library of Wymberley Jones DeRenne. (Savannah, 1911).

_____. "The Brooklyn, New York, Press, 1799-1829," Bulletin of the Bibliographical Society of America, v. 4, nos. 3-4, 1912, p. 37-49.

_____. "William Dunlap and his Writings," Literary Collector, v. 7, 1903-1904, p. 69-76.

Weise, Arthur James. History of the City of Albany, New York. (Albany, 1884).

_____. History of the City of Troy, . . . to . . . 1876. (Troy, 1876).

White, Pliny H. Life and Services of Matthew Lyon. (Burlington, Vt., 1858).

Williams, Robert T. "Pioneer Printers of Old New York," Typothetae Bulletin. August 8, 1927, p. 299-300, 311.

Willyoung, Arthur K. "First American Daily Started 150 Years Ago," American Press, v. 52, no. 12, September, 1934, p. 2, 22.

Winship, George Parker, editor. "French Newspapers in the United States, 1790-1800: The New York Papers," Papers of the Bibliographical Society of America, v. 14, p. 134-141.

_____, editor. "French Newspapers in the United States, 1790-1800: La Patriote Francais, Charleston, 1794-1795," Papers of the Bibliographical Society of America, v. 13, 1919, p. 132-133.

_____, editor. "French Newspapers in the United States, 1790-1800: The Philadelphia Papers," Papers of the Bibliographical Society of America, v. 14, 1920, p. 92-108.

Winterick, John T. "Early American Books and Printing. Chapter V: Gentlemen of the Press (continued)," Publishers' Weekly, v. 123, no. 24, June 17, 1933, p. 1972-1974.

Wright, T. A. "The Newspapers of the County," in William L. Stone, Washington County, New York; Its History . . . (New York, 1901). p. 485-505.

Wroth, Lawrence Counselman. The Colonial Printer. (New York, 1931).

_____. A History of Printing in Colonial Maryland, 1686-1776. (Baltimore, 1922).

With a bibliography of Maryland imprints, 1689-1776.

_____. "A Maryland Proclamation of 1737," in "Notes for Bibliophiles," New York Herald Tribune, October 31, 1926.

Supplemented by "A Correction," in "Notes for Bibliophiles," November 14, 1926.

_____. "Report of the Executors of the Estate of William Parks, the First Printer in Virginia," William and Mary Quarterly, 2d series, v. 2, July, 1922, p. 202-209.

_____. "The St. Mary's City Press, a New Chronology of American Printing," The Colophon, n.s., v. 1, no. 3, / February /, 1936, p. 333-357.

_____. / Note on / "The Will of William Parks / 1750 /, the First Printer in Virginia," William and Mary Quarterly, 2d series, v. 2, April, 1922, p. 92-96.

_____. William Parks, Printer and Journalist of England and Colonial America. (Richmond, 1926).

With a bibliography of William Parks imprints.

Yates, Austin A. Schenectady County, New York; Its History to the Close of the Nineteenth Century. (New York, 1902).

CHRONOLOGICAL CHECKLIST
of BIBLES

LIST OF BIBLES BY DATE

DATE	PRINTER	PLACE	PART, LANGUAGE, ETC.	PAGE
1663	Eliot?		The Indian Bible	70
1688	William Bradford	Philadelphia, Pa.	Proposed, but never printed	5-6
1743	Christopher Saur	Germantown, Pa.	In German	70, 72
1763, 1776	Christopher Saur, Jr.	Germantown, Pa.	In German	74, 75
ca.1776	Christopher Saur	Germantown, Pa.	In German	75
1782	Robert Aitken	Philadelphia, Pa.	Duodecimo	67
1769?	Nicholas Hasselbach	Philadelphia, Pa.	German, unfinished	118
1789	Shelly Arnett	New Brunswick, N.J.	Psalms of David	239
1791, 1793	Isaac Collins	Trenton, N.J.		235
ca.1804	Christopher Saur, Jr.	Baltimore, Md.	Pocket Edition	127-28
1805	Mann & Douglass	Morristown, N.J.		240
?	Benjamin Mecom	?	New Testament, stereotyped, unfinished	46

GEOGRAPHICAL CHECKLIST
of ALMANACS

LIST OF ALMANACS BY LOCATION

PLACE	DATE	PRINTER	TITLE, OTHER DATA	PAGE
Delaware, Wilmington	1761- 1791	James Adams	The Wilmington Almanack, or Ephemeries	245-46, 248
District of Colum- bia, Georgetown	1790	Charles Fierer	Poor Robin's Almanack, or the Maryland Ephemeris	256
District of Colum- bia, Washington	1793	James Doyle	The Potomak Almanack, or, The Washington Ephemeris	258
D.C. Washington	1798	Green, English & Co.		262
D.C. Washington	1801	Rapine, Conrad & Co.	The Washington Repository for the Year 1801	270-71
Maryland, Baltimore	1795-	Samuel Saur	Series, in German	127
Maryland, Frederick	1785	Matthias Bartgis	in German	129
N.J. Morristown	1805-	Jacob Mann	Citizen and Farmer's Almanac. series	240
N.Y. Albany	ca.1788	Charles Webster et al.	series	180
N.Y. Brooklyn	1800	Thomas Kirk	Greenleaf's New-York, Connecticut, & New Jersey Almanack, or Diary	215
N.Y. Hudson	ca.1785	Ashbel Stoddard	Stoddard's Diary, or Col- umbia Almanack. series	191
N.Y. New York	1694	William Bradford		138
N.Y. New York	177-?	Hugh Gaine		159
N.Y. Waterford	1803	Wadsworth & Looker		213
N.C. Edenton	?	William Boylan	Boylan's North Carolina Almanac. series	354
N.C. Fayetteville	1791	Sibley & Howard		360
N.C. Halifax	1795, 1796	Abraham Hodge	Hodge's North-Carolina Almanac	358
Pa. Chestnut Hill	1764	Nicholas Hasselbach	Der Ehrliche Kurtzweiliche Deutsche Americanische Geschichts und Haus Calender	80, 82
Pa. Doylestown	1778?	James Adams		248
Pa. Germantown	1739	Christopher Saur	Der Hoch-Deutsch Americanische Calender	69-70
Pa. Lancaster	1752	James Chattin		78
Pa. Philadelphia	?	Andrew Bradford		16
Pa. Philadelphia	?	Samuel Keimer		17
Pa. Philadelphia	1686	William Bradford	Kalendarium Pennsilvani- ense . . . , by Samuel Atkins	2

PLACE	DATE	PRINTER	TITLE, OTHER DATA	PAGE
Pa. "near Phila delphia"	1687	William Bradford	Almanac by Daniel Leeds	4
Pa. Philadelphia	1688	William Bradford	<u>Almanack</u> by Daniel Leeds	5
Pa. Philadelphia	1688	William Bradford	<u>Almanack</u> by Edward Eaton	5
Pa. Philadelphia	1702-1746	Jacob Taylor, et al.	**series**	12, 13
Pa. Philadelphia	1702	Reynier Jansen	First <u>Almanack</u> by Jacob Taylor	12
Pa. Philadelphia	1705	Tiberius Johnson	A Jacob Taylor <u>Almanack</u>	12
Pa. Philadelphia	1706-1709	?		13
Pa. Philadelphia	1707	Tiberius Johnson	A Jacob Taylor <u>Almanack</u>	12-13
Pa. Philadelphia	1732-	Benjamin Franklin	<u>Poor Richard's Almanacs</u>	34-36, 84
Pa. Philadelphia	1746-	Banjamin Franklin	<u>Neu-Eingerichteter Ameri-canischer Geschichts-Calender.</u> series	47
Pa. P'ttsburgh	1787	Scull & Hall	Proposed only	88
Pa. Pittsburgh	1788	Scull & Boyd	<u>Pittsburg Almanac, or Western Ephemeris</u>	90
Pa. Pittsburgh	1802-	Zadok Cramer	Series	93
Pa. Reading	ca.1789	Gottlob Jungmann	<u>Neuer Hauswirthschafts Calender.</u> series	83
Pa. Washington	1796	Colerick, Hunter & Beaumont		95
Pa. York	1799	Salomon Mayer	<u>Pennsylvanischer Calendar auf das 1799ste Jahr Christi</u>	86
S.C. Charleston	1733	Thomas Whitmarsh		315
Va. Alexandria	1796	Price & Gird	<u>The Gentleman's Political Almanac for 1796</u>	301
Va. Williamsburg	1741-	William Parks, William Hunter, Joseph Royle & Co.	<u>Virginia Almanack.</u> series	284, 286, 288
Va. Williamsburg	1766?-	William Rind	Series	291
Va. Williamsburg	1766	Alexander Purdie & Co.	<u>Virginia Almanack</u>	288
Va. Williamsburg	1769	Purdie & Dixon	<u>Virginia Almanack</u>	288
Jamaica, Kingston	1751	William Daniell		47

GEOGRAPHICAL LIST OF SERIALS MENTIONED IN MCMURTRIE'S HISTORY OF PRINTING

CONNECTICUT
  Danbury
    Republican Journal

  Litchfield
    Weekly Monitor & American
      Advertiser

  New Haven
    Connecticut Gazette

  New London
    Bee

  Norwich
    Norwich Packet

DELAWARE
  Dover
    The Federal Ark
      moved to Wilmington, Del.

  Newcastle
    Newcastle Argus

  Wilmington
    American Watchman
    Christian Repository
    Delaware & Eastern-Shore
      Advertiser
    Delaware Courant
    Delaware Freeman
    Delaware Gazette
    Delaware Gazette (2d)
    Delaware Gazette (3d)
    Delaware Patriot
    Delaware State Journal
    Delaware Statesman
    The Federal Ark
      moved from Dover Del.
    Mirror of the Times
    Monitor
    Museum of Delaware
    Wilmington Courant

DISTRICT OF COLUMBIA
  Georgetown
    Agricultural Museum
    Cabinet
    Centinel, and Country Gazette
    Centinel of Liberty, and George-
      town Advertiser
    Columbian Chronicle
    Columbian Repository
    Federal Republican
      moved from Baltimore, Md.
    Georgetown Museum
    Georgetown Weekly Ledger
    Independent American
    Museum & Georgetown Advertiser
    National Magazine, or Cabinet of
      the United States
    Spirit of Seventy-Six
      moved from Washington, D.C.
    Times, and the Patowmack Packet
    Washington Federalist
    Washington Museum

  Washington
    Alexandria Expositor
      moved from Alexandria, Va.
    American Literary Magazine
      moved to Alexandria, Va.
    Apollo
    Atlantic World
    Colvin's Weekly Register
    Hive, or Repository of Literature
    Impartial Observer, & Washington
      Advertiser
    Monitor
    Museum and Washington and George-
      town Daily Advertiser
    National Intelligencer and Wash-
      ington Advertiser
    Spirit of Seventy-Six
      moved from Richmond, Va.
      moved to Georgetown, D.C.
    Universal Gazette
      moved from Philadelphia, Pa.

Washington, Cont.
  Washington Advertiser
  Washington City Gazette
  Washington Expositor and Weekly
    Intelligencer
  Washington Gazette

FLORIDA
  St. Augustine
    East-Florida Gazette

GEORGIA
  Augusta
    Augusta Chronicle and Gazette
      of the State
    Augusta Herald
    Georgia State Gazette, or
      Independent Register
    Monthly Herald
    Southern Centinel and Universal
      Gazette

  Louisville
    Louisville Gazette and Republican
      Trumpet

  Savannah
    Columbian Museum & Savannah
      Advertiser
    Gazette (unnamed)
    Gazette of the State of Georgia
    Georgia Gazette
    Georgia Gazette (2d)
    Georgia Gazette (3d)
    Georgia Journal and Independent
      Federal Register

KENTUCKY
  Frankfort
    Western World

MARYLAND
  Annapolis
    Maryland Gazette
    Maryland Gazette (2d)
    Maryland Gazette & Annapolis
      Advertiser

Baltimore
  American & Daily Advertiser
  Baltimore Daily Advertiser
  Baltimore Evening Post
  Baltimore Intelligencer
  Baltimore Telegraphe
  Baltimore Weekly Magazine
  Child of Pallas
  City Gazette & Daily Telegraphe
  Daily Intelligencer
  Daily Repository
  Democratic Republican
  Dunlap's Maryland Gazette
  Eagle of Freedom
  Federal Gazette and Baltimore
    Daily Advertiser
  Federal Intelligencer
  Federal Republican
    moved to Georgetown, D.C.
  Maryland Gazette; or the Baltimore
    General Advertiser
  Maryland Journal and Baltimore
    Advertiser
  Neue Unpartheyische Baltimore Bote
    und Marylander Staats-Register
  Niles' Weekly Register
  Palladium of Freedom
  Sunday Monitor
  Telegraphe & Daily Advertiser
  Weekly Museum

Chestertown
  Apollo, or Chestertown Spy
  Chestertown Gazette

Easton
  Maryland Herald and Eastern
    Shore Intelligencer
  Republican Star

Elizabethtown (Hagarstown)
  Maryland Herald
  Washington Spy
  Die Westliche Correspondenz

Fredericktown (Frederick)
Bartgis's Federal Gazette
Bartgis's Maryland Gazette
Bartgis's Republican Gazette
Frederick-Town Herald
Der General Staatsbote
Maryland Chronicle
Maryland Gazette
Rights of Man

Hagarstown, see
Elizabethtown

Rockville
Maryland Register

MASSACHUSETTS
Boston
Herald of Freedom and the
Federal Advertiser
Massachusetts Gazette
New-England Courant
New-England Magazine

Salem
Salem Gazette

Stockbridge
Western Star

NEW JERSEY
Bridgeton
Argus
Plain Dealer

Burlington
Burlington Advertiser
New-Jersey Gazette
moved to Trenton, N.J.
New-Jersey Magazine

Chatham
New-Jersey Journal

Elizabethtown (Elizabeth)
Christian's Scholar's and
Farmer's Magazine
Elizabeth Daily Journal

Elizabethtown, cont.
New-Jersey Journal
Political Intelligencer
moved from New Brunswick, N.J.

Morristown
Genius of Liberty
Morris County Gazette
Morris-Town Herald
Palladium of Liberty

Mt. Pleasant
Jersey Chronicle

New Brunswick
Arnett's New Jersey Federalist
Brunswick Gazette
Genius of Liberty
New Brunswick Gazette
New Jersey Federalist
Political Intelligencer
moved to Elizabethtown, N.J.

Newark
Centinel of Freedom
New-York Gazette & the Weekly
Mercury
moved from New York, N.Y.
Newark Gazette
Newark Republican Herald
Woods's Newark Gazette

Newton
Farmer's Journal & Newton
Advertiser

Princeton
Princeton Packet

Trenton
Federal Post
New-Jersey Gazette
moved from Burlington, N.J.
New Jersey State Gazette
New Jersey State Gazette (2d)
State Gazette
Trenton Mercury

Woodbridge
  Constitutional Courant
  New American Magazine

NEW YORK
  Albany
    Albany Argus
    Albany Centinel
    Albany Chronicle
    Albany Gazette
    Albany Gazette (2d)
    Albany Journal
    Albany Register
    Balance, and New York State
      Journal
    Federal Herald
      moved to Lansingburgh, N.Y.
    Freemason's Monitor
    New York Gazetteer, or Northern
      Intelligencer
    Northern Centinel
      moved from Lansingburgh, N.Y.
    Plough Boy
    Republican Crisis

  Athens
    Monitor

  Auburn
    Advocate of the People

  Ballston Spa
    Independent American
    Republican Telescope
    Rural Visitor & Saratoga
      Advertiser
    Saratoga Advertiser
    Saratoga Courier
    Saratoga Journal
    Saratoga Patriot
    Saratoga Register: or, Farmer's
      Journal
    Saratoga Republican

  Brooklyn
    Brooklyn Minerva and Long Island
      Advertiser
    Long Island Courier

Brooklyn, cont.
  Long Island Star
  Long Island Weekly Intelligencer
  Young Misses Magazine

Caldwell
  Lake George Watchman

Cambridge
  Cambridge Gazette

Canaan
  Columbian Mercury

Catskill
  American Eagle
  Catskill Packet
  Catskill Recorder
  Disseminator
  Greene & Delaware Washingtonian
  Western Constellation

Elizabethtown
  Essex Patriot
  Reveille

Fishkill
  New York Packet
    moved from New York, N.Y.

Glen's Falls
  Adviser
  Warren Republican

Goshen
  Goshen Repository & Weekly
    Intelligencer
  Independent Republican
    moved from Montgomery, N.Y.
  Orange County Gazette
    moved to Newburgh, N.Y.
  Orange County Patriot
  Orange County Republican
  Orange Eagle
  Orange Patrol

Hudson
  Balance
  Balance Advertiser
  Balance and Columbia Repository
  Bee
  Columbia Magazine
  Columbia Republican
  Hudson Weekly Gazette
  Northern Whig
  Republican Fountain
  Wasp

Kingston
  Farmer's Register
  Plebian
  Rising Sun
  Ulster County Gazette
  Ulster Gazette

Lansingburgh
  American Spy
  Farmer's Oracle & Lansingburgh
    Weekly Gazette
    moved to Troy, N.Y.
  Farmers' Register
    moved to Troy, N.Y.
  Federal Herald
    moved from Albany, N.Y.
  Lansingburgh Gazette
  Lansingburgh Recorder
  Northern Budget
    moved to Troy, N.Y.
  Northern Centinel
    moved to Albany, N.Y.
  Recorder
    moved to Troy, N.Y.
  Tiffany's Recorder

Montgomery
  Independent Republican
    moved to Goshen, N.Y.

Mt. Pleasant
  Impartial Gazette
  Westchester Herald
  Westchester Patriot

New Windsor
  New-Windsor Gazette

New York
  American Chronicle
  American Citizen
  American Magazine
  Bee
  Constitutional Gazette
  Daily Advertiser
  Diary
  Independent Journal: or, The
    General Advertiser
  Independent New-York Gazette
  Independent Reflector
  Instructor
  John Englishman
  Minerva
  New York Chronicle
  New-York Columbian
  New-York Daily Gazette
  New-York Evening Post
  New-York Evening Post (2d)
  New-York Gazette
  New York Gazette (2d)
  New York Gazette (3d)
  New-York Gazette & the Weekly
    Mercury
    moved to Newark, N.J.
  New-York Gazette; or, The Weekly
    Post-Boy
  New York Gazetteer, and Country
    Journal
  New-York Journal or General
    Advertiser
  New York Mercury
  New York Mercury (2d)
  New York Morning Post
  New York Morning Post and Daily
    Advertiser
  New York Packet
    moved to Fishkill, N.Y.
  New York Pacquet
  New-York Weekly Journal
  New-York Weekly Post Boy
  Plebian
  Republican Watch-Tower
  Rivington's New-York Gazette
  Rivington's New-York Gazetteer;
    or the Connecticut, New-Jersey
    Hudson's-River, and Quebec
    Weekly Advertiser

New York, cont.
  Royal American Gazette
  Royal Gazette
  Time Piece
  Watch Tower

Newburg (Newburgh)
  Mirror
  Newburgh Packet
  Newburgh Republican
  Orange County Gazette
    moved from Goshen, N.Y.
  Orange County Gazette (2d)
  Orange County Gazette, and
    Newburgh Public Advertiser
  Orange County Patriot: or, The
    Spirit of Seventy-Six
  Political Index
  Recorder of the Times
  Rights of Man

Otsego
  Otsego Herald

Plattsburg
  American Monitor
  Clinton Advertisor
  Northern Herald
  Political Observatory
  Republican

Poughkeepsie
  American Farmer
  Country Journal, and the
    Poughkeepsie Advertiser
  Dutchess Observer
  Farmer
  Northern Politician
  Political Barometer
  Poughkeepsie Journal
  Poughkeepsie Journal and Con-
    stitutional Republican
  Republican Herald
  Republican Journal
  Rural Casket

Sag Harbor, L.I.
  American Eagle
  Frothingham's Long Island
    Herald
  Suffolk County Herald
  Suffolk County Recorder
  Suffolk Gazette

Salem
  Northern Centinel
  Northern Post
  Times, or National Courier
  Washington County Post
  Washington Patrol
  Washington Register

Saratoga Springs
  Saratoga Gazette
  Saratoga Sentinel

Schenectady
  Cabinet
  Mohawk Advertiser
  Mohawk Mercury
  Pastime
  Schenectady Gazette
  Western Budget
  Western Spectator

Troy
  Farmer's Oracle
    moved from Lansingburgh, N.Y.
  Farmers' Register
    moved from Lansingburgh, N.Y.
  Northern Budget
    moved from Lansingburgh, N.Y.
  Recorder
    moved from Lansingburgh, N.Y.
  Tiffany's Recorder
    moved from Lansingburgh, N.Y.
  Troy Gazette
  Troy Post

Upton
  Columbian Courier

Wardsbridge
 Orange County Republican

Waterford
 Waterford Gazette

Whitestown
 Whitestown Gazette

NORTH CAROLINA
 Edenton
  Edenton Gazette
  Edenton Gazette (2d)
  Edenton Intelligencer
  Encyclopedian Instructor
  Herald of Freedom
  Post-Angel
  State Gazette of North Carolina
   moved from Newbern, N.C.

 Fayetteville
  American
  Carolina Observer
  Fayetteville Gazette
  Fayetteville Gazette (2d)
  North Carolina Centinel
  North Carolina Chronicle
  North Carolina Intelligencer
  North Carolina Journal
  North-Carolina Minerva
   moved to Raleigh, N.C.

 Halifax
  North-Carolina Journal

 Hillsborough (Hillsboro)
  Hillsborough Recorder
  North Carolina Gazette

 New Bern (Newbern)
  Carolina Centinel
  Carolina Federal Republican
  Newbern Gazette
  Newbern Herald
  North Carolina Circular
  North Carolina Gazette
  North Carolina Gazette (2d)
  North Carolina Magazine

New Bern, cont.
 State Gazette of North Carolina
  moved from Edenton, N.C.
 True Republican

Raleigh
 Minerva
 North-Carolina Minerva
  moved from Fayetteville, N.C.
 Raleigh Register

Salisbury
 North Carolina Mercury
 Western Carolinian

Wilmington
 Cape-Fear Herald
 Cape-Fear Mercury
 Cape-Fear Recorder
 Hall's Wilmington Gazette
 North-Carolina Gazette and Weekly
  Post-Boy
 True Republican
 Wilmington Centinel
 Wilmington Chronicle
 Wilmington Gazette

OHIO
 Chillicothe
  Scioto Gazette

PENNSYLVaNIA
 Beaver
  Minerva

 Brownsville
  Brownsville Gazette

 Carlisle
  Carlisle Gazette
  Eagle, or, Carlisle Herald
  Telegraphe
  Times

 Chambersburg
  Western Advertiser

Chestnut Hill
  Chesnuthiller Wochenschrift

Connellsville
  Herald

Easton
  Neuer Unpartheyischer Eastoner
    Bothe

Erie
  Mirror

Germantown
  Ein Geistliches Magazien
  Germantowner Zeitung
  Hoch-Deutsch Pennsylvanische
    Geschicht-Schreiber
  Pennsylvanische-Berichte

Greensburg
  Farmers' Register

Hanover
  Die Pennsylvanische Wochenschrift

Harrisburg
  Harrisburger Morgenröthe

Indiana
  American

Lancaster
  Der Americanische Staatsbothe
  Der Deutsche Porcupein
  Lancaster Correspondent
  Lancaster Journal
  Lancaster Wochenblatt
  Lancasterische Zeitung
  Das Landsmanns Wochenblatt
  Neue Unpartheyische Lancaster
    Zeitung
  Pennsylvania Packet
    moved from Philadelphia, Pa.
  Das Pennsylvanische Zeitungs-Blat

Meadville
  Crawford Weekly Messenger

Mercer
  Western Press

Perryopolis
  Comet

Philadelphia
  All the News for Two Coppers
  Allied Mercury
  American Daily Advertiser
  American Magazine
  American Magazine and Monthly
    Chronicle
  American Magazine, or General
    Repository
  American Weekly Mercury
  Aurora
  Carey's United States Recorder
  Constitutional Diary
  Courier de l'Amerique
  Daily Advertiser
  Gales's Independent Gazetteer
  Gemeinüt"zige Philadelphische
    Correspondenz
  General Magazine And Historical
    Chronicle, For all the British
    Plantations in America
  General Post-Bothe
  High-Dutch and English Gazette
    (or)
  Hoch Teutsche und Englische
    Zeitung
  Independent Gazetteer
  Merchants' Daily Advertiser
  Minerva
  National Gazette
  Neue Philadelphische Correspondenz
  Pelosi's Marine List
  Pennsylvania Chronicle and Univer-
    sal Advertiser
  Pennsylvania Evening Post
  Pennsylvania Evening Post, and
    Daily Advertiser
  Pennsylvania Gazette
    moved to York, Pa.
  Pennsylvania Journal
  Pennsylvania Ledger
  Pennsylvania Packet
    moved to Lancaster, Pa.

Philadelphia, cont.
Pennsylvania Staats Courier
Die Pennsylvanische Gazette
Penny Post
Philadelphier Teutsche Fama
Das Philadelphier Wochenblatt
Philadelphische Zeitung
Philadelphische Zeitung; von
   allerhand Auswartig und einheim-
   ischen merckwurdigen Sachen
Philadelphisches Staatsregister
Story & Humphrey's Pennsylvania
   Mercury
Universal Gazette
   moved to Washington, D.C.
Universal Instructor in all Arts
   and Sciences: and Pennsylvania
   Gazette
Weekly Price Current
Der Wochentliche Philadelphische
   Staatsbote

Pittsburgh
Commonwealth
Mercury
Navigator
   or
Ohio Navigator
Pittsburgh Gazette
Statesman
Tree of Liberty

Reading
Neue Unpartheyische Readinger
   Zeitung
Readinger Adler
Readinger Zeitung
Der Unpartheyische Reading Adler
Weekly Advertiser

Sunbury
Freiheitsvogel

Uniontown
Fayette Gazette
Genius of Liberty
Western Register
   moved from Washington, Pa.

Washington
Herald of Liberty
Reporter
Washingtonian
Western Corrector
Western Register
   moved to Uniontown, Pa.
Western Telegraphe

Waynesburgh
Messenger

York
Pennsylvania Chronicle
Pennsylvania Gazette
   moved from Philadelphia
Pennsylvania Herald
Unpartheyische York Gazette

RHODE ISLAND
Providence
Providence Gazette

SOUTH CAROLINA
Camden
Camden Intelligencer
Camden Journal

Charleston
Carolina Gazette
Charleston Courier
Charleston Evening Gazette
Charleston Evening Post
Charleston Gazette
Charleston Morning Post
Chronicle of Liberty
City Gazette
Columbian Herald; or, the New
   Daily Advertiser
Columbian Herald, or the Patri-
   otic Courier of North America
Daily Evening Gazette and Charles-
   ton Tea-Table Companion
Evening Courier
Evening Post & General
   Advertiser
Federal Carolina Gazette

Charleston, cont.
  Gazette of the State of South
    Carolina
  Royal Gazette
  Royal South-Carolina Gazette
  South-Carolina and American
    General Gazette
  South Carolina Gazette
  South Carolina Gazette (2d)
  South Carolina Gazette; and
    Country Journal
  South Carolina Gazette and
    General Advertiser
  South-Carolina State-Gazette
  South Carolina Weekly Advertiser
  South Carolina Weekly Gazette
  South Carolina Weekly Journal
  Star: and Charleston Daily
    Advertiser
  State Gazette of South-Carolina
  Telegraphe: and Charleston
    Daily Advertiser
  Times and Political and Commer-
    cial Evening Gazette

Columbia
  Columbia Gazette
  South Carolina Gazette
  State Gazette of South Carolina

Georgetown
  Georgetown Chronicle
  Georgetown Gazette
  South Carolina Independent
    Gazette; and Georgetown
    Chronicle

Statesburg
  Claremont Gazette

VIRGINIA
  Abbingdon
    Holston Intelligencer

  Alexandria
    Alexandria Advertiser
    Alexandria Daily Gazette
    Alexandria Expositor
      moved to Washington, D.C.

Alexandria, cont.
  Alexandria Times
  American Literary Magazine
    moved from Washington, D.C.
  Columbian Advertiser
  Columbian Mirror
  Times of Alexandria
  Virginia Gazette
  Virginia Gazette and Alexandria
    Advertiser
  Virginia Journal

Charlottesville
  Central Gazette

Dumfries
  Republican Journal
  Virginia Gazette
  Virginia Gazette and Agricultural
    Depository

HMS Dunmore
  Virginia Gazette

Fincastle
  Fincastle Weekly Advertiser
  Herald of Virginia

Fredericksburg
  Courier
  Genius of Liberty
  Republican Citizen
  Virginia Herald

Leesburg
  Genius of Liberty
  Impartial Journal
  Republican Press
  True American
  Washingtonian

Lexington
  Rockbridge Repository

Lynchburg
  Lynchburg Weekly Gazette
  Lynchburg Weekly Museum
  Union Gazette

Newmarket
  Virginische Volksberichier, und
    Newmarketen Wochenschrift

Norfolk
  American Gazette
  Commercial Register
  Norfolk & Portsmouth Chronicle
  Norfolk & Portsmouth Gazette
  Norfolk & Portsmouth Journal
  Norfolk Gazette
  Norfolk Herald
  Virginia Chronicle
  Virginia Gazette
  Virginia Gazette, or Norfolk
    Intelligencer

Petersburg
  Independent Ledger
  Petersburg Intelligencer
  Republican
  Virginia Gazette
  Virginia Star

Richmond
  Examiner
  Friend of the People
  National Magazine
  Observatory
  Richmond & Manchester Advertiser
  Spirit of Seventy-Six
    moved to Washington, D.C.
  Virginia Argus
  Virginia Federalist
  Virginia Gazette
  Virginia Gazette
    moved from Williamsburg, Va.
  Virginia Gazette & General
    Advertiser
  Virginia Gazette & Independent
    Chronicle
  Virginia Gazette, and Public
    Advertiser
  Virginia Gazette and Richmond and
    Manchester Advertiser
  Virginia Gazette & Richmond
    Chronicle

Richmond, cont.
  Virginia Gazette: and Richmond
    Daily Advertiser
  Virginia Gazette & Weekly
    Advertiser
  Virginia Independent Chronicle
  Virginia Patriot

Staunton
  Phenix
  Political Mirror
  Scourge of Aristocracy
  Staunton Spy
  Virginia Gazette

Westchester
  Philanthropist

Williamsburg
  Virginia Gazette
  Virginia Gazette (2d)
  Virginia Gazette (3d)
    moved to Richmond, Va.
  Virginia Gazette (4th)
  Virginia Miscellany

Winchester
  Independent Register
  Virginia Centinel
  Virginia Gazette
  Willis's Virginia Gazette
  Winchester Triumph of Liberty

Wythe Court House
  Republican Luminary

BAHAMA ISLAND
  Nassau
    Royal Bahama Gazette

CANADA
  New Brunswick
    Royal St. John's Gazette

  Nova Scotia
    Nova Scotia Packet: and General
      Advertiser

Quebec
> Gazette de Montreal
> Gazette de Quebec
> La Gazette du Commerce et
>   Litteraire
> Montreal Gazette

ENGLAND
> London
> > London Evening Post
>
> Ludlow
> > The Ludlow Post-Man
>
> Reading
> > Reading Mercury, or Weekly
> >   Entertainer
>
> Sheffield
> > Sheffield Register

FRANCE
> Passy
> > Supplement to the Boston
> >   Independent Chronicle

WEST INDIES
> Antigua
> > Antigua Gazette
>
> Jamaica, Kingston
> > Jamaica Courant
> > Jamaica Mercury
> > Royal Gazette